For my mother and father

FRANCIS

THE JOURNEY
AND THE DREAM

Murray Bodo

ST. ANTHONY MESSENGER PRESS

Cincinnati, Ohio

Nihil Obstat:	Rev. Hilarion Kistner, O.F.M.
	Rev. Edward Gratsch
Imprimi Potest:	Rev. Jeremy Harrington, O.F.M.
	Provincial
Imprimatur:	+ James H. Garland, V.G.
	Archdiocese of Cincinnati
	August 16, 1988

The *nihil obstat* and *imprimatur* are a declaration that a book or pamphlet is considered to be free from doctrinal and moral error. It is not implied that those who have granted the *nihil obstat* and *imprimatur* agree with the contents, opinions or statements expressed.

Cover design by Mark Sullivan
Book design by Julie Lonneman
Illustrations by Lawrence Zink

ISBN-13: 978-0-86716-116-8
ISBN-10: 0-86716-116-7

Published by St. Anthony Messenger Press
28 W. Liberty St.
Cincinnati, OH 45202
www.AmericanCatholic.org

Printed in the U.S.A.
Printed on acid-free paper

07 08 09 14 13 12 11

Preface to the New Edition

The hill behind the fortress they call the Rocca Maggiore is covered again this year with ginestra, Umbria's omnipresent broom plant. And they are still quarrying pink Assisi stone from that same hillside. Across the valley where the river Tescio runs quietly, there is the large field of poppies that I expect to see each summer but always surprises me with its brilliance the first time I come around the bend in the road just beyond the cemetery.

It is a clear day in early June: a cool breeze is blowing softly from the direction of Mount Subasio. I stop at a small cliff just outside the cemetery and look out across another valley to the great Basilica of St. Francis. There are poppies at my feet, red with all the suffering of Francis, the *Poverello* whose body lies interred beneath the weight of all that stone. I sit on a broken column and remember my first view of the basilica from here 16 years ago on a cold and damp morning in late March.

From where I sit I can see to my left only one tower of the Rocca Maggiore. The final lines for this morning's Mass leap into my mind: "...It is a narrow gate and a hard road that leads to life, and only a few find it" (Mt. 7:14). Francis' narrow gate was the gate on the opposite side of the city from where I sit looking at the western tower of the Rocca Maggiore. Through that gate he left the safety of Assisi and walked down the hill toward the leper colony that lay near the little Church of the Portiuncula, the Little Portion, as it was affectionately named.

St. Francis, when I wrote the pages of this book and even now so many years later, is for me the man who walked through the narrow gate of his city, leaving behind possessions, mother and father, friends and relatives, and began to live among the lepers a free and unfettered life that transformed the fetid swamp below Assisi into a new Eden, a paradise of Christian love. That image has remained with me, and that image made this book a joy for me to write.

Writing is usually hard for me: heavy the words, heavy their making on the page. But *Francis: The Journey and the Dream* flowed easily. I felt, as I penned these words, that someone else was writing them. It was the closest thing I've ever experienced to the muse that poets speak of. I believe that St. Francis himself was my muse, that his was the freshness of these words, of this vision. And therefore in this new edition I have changed nothing of that original Dream. I have only tried to make the language more all-inclusive and less sexist. When I first penned these words in 1972, I was not aware of how chauvinistic some of my language was. Since then I've grown more sensitive to the importance of all-inclusive language, a gift from those other muses, the women of my life. To them and to Mary, the Mother of God, Clare of Assisi and Therese of Lisieux, I dedicate this edition of *Francis: The Journey and the Dream.*

Murray Bodo, O.F.M.
Assisi
June 21, 1988

Contents

vii

Introduction

There is a large plain in the center of Italy in the province of Umbria that breathes the peace of one man, a perfectly free and unfettered spirit who was born in the small town of Assisi in the year 1182. The world knows him as the saint and poet and little poor man, Francis of Assisi. Even today, as you walk through the Umbrian countryside, the peace of St. Francis seeps into your soul and you begin to believe again that perfect joy is possible even for modern men and women on the same terms that Francis won it. These terms most would consider too high, for Francis won peace and joy through perfect detachment.

The following is a pilgrim's account of what that detachment involved. The story begins and ends with the death of Francis. Everything in between is memory and therefore the incidents are fragmentary and without a continuous thread of narrative. Its unity is, I hope, Francis himself.

These pages are not a biography of St. Francis. For that kind of book I have neither the background nor the inclination. I have merely tried to share my personal view of St. Francis, and, in the process, a new Francis, a Francis I did not know, has emerged.

Finally, I would like to express my gratitude to Father Jeremy Harrington, who asked me to write this book, to Father Roger Huser, my Provincial Minister, who encouraged me all along the way, and to all my Franciscan Brothers whose good example has inspired my own Dream and made my Journey possible.

A Journey of Dreams

He lay in the grip of his last fever, the bright points of pain stabbing into his back, and he knew that this was the beginning of what he had dreamed of so long: "Lord, lead my soul out of prison." Earlier that day his brothers had carried him here to this chapel of Our Lady of the Angels, on the plain below the city. As they made the steep descent from Assisi, Francis had asked them to stop at the leper colony, so that from there he could bless his town for the last time. He was almost blind, but he thought he could see the city stretched out before him like a wide, multicolored tapestry. Perhaps he saw it only with his spirit.

How different the town looked today from what it was that day years before when he had risen from his long illness and staggered about the green hills and found that they no longer lifted his heart. He was only 22 years old then. It had been a bright day, and he remembered the roofs catching the sun like quilts of red and pink and white. But their beauty had only depressed him. The heavy spirit of melancholy had him in her grip, and he didn't understand, didn't want to understand why.

People who passed the young Francis as he trudged up the long hill had recognized him and congratulated him that he was well again. And he remembered thinking cynically: They are saying to themselves, "There's Pietro's worthless son. He looks pretty pale, shaky on his feet, too. But why should we worry about it? He's better off than we'll ever be. At least he has a future."

If only they had known the emptiness and despair he suffered precisely because he *was* Pietro Bernardone's son, precisely because he *was* rich and famous and well-liked. How terribly boring it all seemed then. And yet somehow when he looked back at the city from the top of Mount Subasio, he was still young enough at 22 to believe that some destiny was waiting for him that would make that lovely city proud of him. Where and when the call to destiny waited for him, he did not know, but his

3

deepest suspicion was that he would finally respond to the call of chivalry that plagued him night and day, and become a knight. That had to be where his future lay...

The pains in his head and chest and back started again and Francis was jerked momentarily from his reverie. He coughed deeply and clutched his cross more tightly. The pains were beginning to dull his senses, and he slowly slipped back into his memories of the past...

That day, 23 years before, as he stood on the hill outside his town, he had experienced the great disillusionment of his youth. He had suddenly realized that in his illness something very sad had happened to him. He would surely have despaired then and given up hope of ever being happy again were it not for the Dream. A few weeks after he had stood despondent on Mount Subasio, wondering if his brief 22 years were the end of life and of youth, he dreamed the Dream that changed everything forever.

The Dream

Francis tossed in his bed, straining his mind, begging it to relax, asking it to sleep, coaxing his body gently, then violently, to drop off into slumber.

"Quit thinking. Please sleep, mind. I have to rest, to sleep, or I'll never recover from this madness, this despair that's clutching at me here in the dark." He got up and paced the room, his hands ruffling his tangled black hair.

"What's the matter with me? This is so crazy. How can I be afraid and upset when there is nothing to be afraid of? It's so silly. Get back into bed, Francis. Relax."

He dove onto the bed and lay face down, trying to feel exhausted, but he couldn't sleep. All night he tossed and sweated and asked himself why sleep never came easily anymore. It had been this way since his illness and the strange feeling of loneliness he'd experienced walking the hills of Assisi that first day he dared leave his sickbed and venture outside into the sun. Now his nights were filled with terror and preciously snatched moments of half-sleep.

Finally, when the first rays of morning were streaking across his bare back, Francis dozed off. And then it was he had the Dream.

He was led into the great hall of a dazzling Palace, where a radiant Princess-Bride held court. The walls were covered with shields and trophies of battles won. And when he asked aloud who the Lord of the castle was, a voice sang out: "It's the high court of Francis Bernardone and his followers."

When Francis awoke, something had changed. It was not the message of the Dream that moved him so, not the announcement that he was going to be a great lord. No, it was the *fact* of the Dream, that it had happened, that he now had a sense of direction, something to live for. There was a certainty about his Dream, like that of a vision. Even had the Dream been of Francis' losing his money and position and becoming a beggar, it would have pleased him, because then he would at least have known which way to go. A sense of goal and purpose were more important, it seemed, than what direction he was going in. Maybe it had something to do with his own worth or who he was, but most of all, it meant that he was *going* somewhere, anywhere. His will was no longer paralyzed, the dream had freed him from his own frozen will.

So Francis had determined to make his Dream come true, knowing that it was the setting-out that mattered. He remembered so clearly his lightness of heart as he left Assisi to join the papal armies of Walter of Brienne, the Norman captain who was winning brilliant battles in the service of Pope Innocent III. But the pattern of highs and lows in his life wasn't to be altered so easily, even by visions and dreams. He'd only been on the road a day or so when, in the city of Spoleto, he began again to hear voices in the night.

5

Dream at Spoleto

"Francis, is it better to serve the Lord or the servant?"

"Oh, sir, the Lord, of course."

"Then, why are you trying to turn your Lord into a servant?"
And Francis, trembling in recognition, replied, "Lord, what
do You want me to do?"

"Go home, Francis, and think about your first vision. You
have seen only the appearances and not the heart of glory and
fame. You are trying to make your vision fit your own impatient
desire for Knighthood."

And Francis, shaken and fully awake, understood now that
he had taken too much into his own hands. He realized that
impatience had driven him to act too quickly and that he must
wait and listen and purify his heart to hear deeper words than
he had imagined. He had tried to make God's will serve his own
impatient desire for glory. He had not really listened.

The road back to Assisi seemed to shake beneath him. As a
knightly figure returning home alone, he seem to shout, "I am
retreating," for the world to hear. But he didn't mind the quizzical
looks and the scorn on the faces of the peasants who stared at
him. Somehow, that was how it should be now. He should, in fact,
be walking as they were, and not sitting on a magnificent war
horse.

He was returning to Assisi on the Roman Flaminian Way.
The Roman legions had marched this same way, bold and
confident of the power of Rome. They stopped and drank from
the sacred spring of Clitunno near Foligno. They asked the water
nymphs there to strengthen them in battle, to give them courage
and victory.

As Francis passed that same clear pool of water, the dream
of glory drained from his heart, and war and victory were empty
words rattling in his brain. He felt empty. Something told him he
was leaving the Roman way forever.

A New Birth

Francis' unexpected return from Spoleto was the most terrible experience of his early life. The utter scorn of Assisi's citizens drove him into himself as nothing before had ever done. The rumor of his supposed cowardice swept through the city like a wind-fanned fire. Some suspected that two years before when he had been taken prisoner at Ponte San Giovanni, he had actually surrendered himself out of fear. Others pointed out that the long illness after his release from prison at Perugia was really guilt and remorse for what he done.

His father, Pietro, was crestfallen. He loved Francis dearly, and he did not believe that his son was a coward, but he was hard put to explain why Francis had returned from Spoleto. His mother, Lady Pica, grieved terribly for him and longed to soothe the secret spot of his hurt, but she did not know how. And Francis himself tried desperately to explain, but he only further convinced his parents that he had not fully recovered from the strange melancholy and delusions of his illness.

Francis walked the streets of Assisi in a daze. He lived in constant guilt, wondering, as he trudged along, if his cheeks were flushed with shame. His friends were away with the army of Walter of Brienne; and he alone, among the able young men, remained behind with women and children and older men who had long since proven themselves in battle. Yet he knew he could not return to battle, for that would only prove what everyone suspected: that he was a coward and had finally recovered his nerve.

To listen to one's own heart when others are saying something different is the hardest test of one's spirit. And Francis thought he would not survive it. He prayed as he had never prayed before, begging Jesus to tell him why He had asked him to return to Assisi. But there was no answer.

During these long, terrifying months, Francis used to go to a little cave in the hill opposite Mount Subasio and try to think out what was happening to him. He went to the cave every day until it became a home for him, the only place in which he felt comfortable. And he came to think of himself as a man acquainted with the dark holes of the earth. It was there in the womb of the mountain that he finally found peace of heart and the courage to stand upright again. It was there that he was born again.

The Cave

Softly speaking into the dark cave's ear, Francis experienced the parched joy of release. The protective shield of dark made it easier to whisper hushed secrets into the emptiness, or to scream his pain at the cold damp walls.

Every day it became harder to leave his cave and meet the harsh light of all the staring world. The farther into the cave he retreated, the more comfortably insulated he felt.

"Lord Jesus, let me stay here; let me hide in the womb of this wet earth sponging me in soft, gentle mud."

But every day he was driven outside again by the panic that the light would not be there to blind him. "O womb of earth, hide me from eyes that freeze me into this paralyzing fear."

It was in the cave that Francis met Jesus and saw himself for the first time. Up to that time his voices and dreams always seemed to come from without, from a great distance. But during the agonizing hours in the cave, he began to hear a voice inside himself, a deeper, clearer voice that was like discovering a part of himself he did not know was there. The more he prayed and turned to Christ for inspiration, the deeper he plunged toward some inner force that gave him strength and peace. He stopped talking to the bare walls of the cave.

At first, this inner search was a painful and terrifying look at himself, at his weakness and sinfulness; and the journey was a downward dive that made him feel that he was drowning in some vast, bottomless lake. But as he persevered in prayer, he came at last to something like a great, silent waterproof cavern in which the sound of his own voice seemed mellow and deep; and there at that depth within, Jesus spoke softly to him and made his heart burn with love. Afterwards he would soar to the surface again, renewed and encouraged. But each time he had to make the painful and frightening dive. And each time he was afraid he would not be able to find the cavern again.

During that whole year after hearing the voice of Christ at Spoleto, Francis went to the cave outside Assisi, and plumbed his own depths trying to bring that inner cave-peace to the surface permanently. In the end, he sensed somehow that the search for the cavern would be his daily journey the rest of his life; and if he was to be at peace, he would have to delve deeply in prayer every day. That thought gave him great joy, because he had come to love the quest and the fear and the anticipation as a part of the whole process of praying and listening to Christ.

Of Loneliness

Watching from a corner of the piazza Francis could see the young girl's face, and he grieved at the sadness in the eyes. So young and lovely and so terribly alone in her anguish. He could see only the back of her boyfriend's head, but that was enough to give him a picture of the boy's pained expression. Something had happened between them or inside them that made their standing together strained. Francis knew the kind of feeling he saw in the girl's eyes. It was so choked and suppressed under her outward control that he felt the constriction in his own chest. It pained him so, to be unable to help, but it would have been totally tasteless for him to interfere and he dropped his eyes to the cobblestoned piazza.

Almost immediately, his eyes rested again on the girl. Someday, perhaps soon, he would find what he was looking for. It wasn't closeness, really, or the touch of another person, but it had something to do with that girl and his need to comfort her, to feel her head on his shoulder and to know that she was happy and secure beside him.

Or was it his own security he was thinking about? He didn't think so, and "security" was perhaps not the right word for what was troubling him. Now that he had heard his voices and this new dimension had come into his life, he felt alone. The only real relationship in his life was with his voices and dreams. They had become the real world, and what he saw and heard and touched with his senses was ever fading and dissolving like smoke. Even in his imagination, the girl would dissolve as soon as she rested her head on his shoulder, and he was alone again.

Francis wondered whether a real girl, this girl, would also dissolve if he touched her. Or, if she did not, would his dreams and voices dissolve? He was afraid to try and touch anyone. The dreams had won, the feeling of loneliness would remain.

Lady Poverty

Francis, shaken loose from his boyhood companions, resembled a pathetic leader self-exiled from his people. He stood at the corners of streets and spied around buildings at the carefree life of his former days. Alone, on evenings especially, he yearned to return and discard his dreams as the illusions of an ambitious and frustrated idealist. But just as he would start toward his former companions, a panic would clutch at his heart that he was throwing away some jewel or treasure of incomparable beauty and value. And he couldn't do it. Though he longed for companionship, he somehow felt in the marrow of himself that there were new companions just around the next dream.

And if there weren't? What then? Could he endure this kind of loneliness for a phantom lady, the lady of his original Dream, the lady of his Dream-castle, a lady he never really saw or touched? The prospect was frightening and made him feel timid and insecure. After all, only *he* heard the voices and dreamed the dreams, and hadn't he been ill and weak for so long? Perhaps the dreams were only his strong desire for recognition taking on flesh in a world of fantasy and self-deception. Like the Prophet Daniel he was a man of desires, impatient for their fulfillment, drunk on his own importance.

That thought always made him laugh: an important man, a knight or hero from Assisi! Who ever heard of Assisi? A 13th-century cliff dwelling clinging for dear life to the side of Mount Subasio. Some day the mountain would shake its side and the whole town would come tumbling down into the valley.

And yet, try as he may, he could not shake the Dream, and the voices became more real than those of the people in the piazza.

He would have despaired over the voices' stubborn ringing in his ears, were it not for the indescribable peace that they had brought to his life. Even now as he lingered at the edge of deserted streets, looking down their black tunnels to the light of the town square beyond, the peace that lay deep within soothed somewhat the lonely feeling of having no one to share his dreams with.

In prayer, he did speak tenderly with Jesus, but that was not the same. He wanted some companion, some friend he could see and reach out to and know that he was heard and understood. Perhaps he wanted too much; inner peace of heart and the love of God, and human companionship as well. But hadn't God said that it was not good for us to be alone? Something that stirred in his consciousness—and seemed to come in muffled tones from the beginning of time—said that he would never and could never be a hermit. The Gospel, always the Gospel life, moved him. Not Christ alone, but Christ and his disciples, Jesus of Nazareth and his little band of followers, witnessing together the "foolishness" and goodness of God.

One man alone was a poor sign of love. People saw love in *people* who love, in people whose relationship with one another radiated a higher than human love. A family of brothers caring about one another and witnessing to the world that love is possible would be like a rebirth of the primitive Church that led the Romans to say, "See how these Christians love one another."

But now he was alone, a single, solitary man. What *did* always console and encourage him, though, was that in his first dream there had been many shields on the walls of the castle. Surely they were not all to be his. They belonged to others who would join him some day, others who would come under the spell of his lady. From his sojourn in the cave, he now knew that this lady was symbolic of the poor Christ, of chastity, of valor and courage, of chivalry and virtue and everything spiritual and fine. But most of all she was Lady Poverty. To serve her was all his desire. Lady Poverty! To serve her was to be rich beyond imagining.

Lady Poverty was *the* symbol of the paradoxes of the Gospel: richness in poverty, life in death, strength in weakness, beauty in the sordid and shabby, peace in conflict and temptation, fullness in emptiness and, above all, love in detachment and deprivation. She made everything hard soft, and everything difficult easy.

11

If Lady Poverty were true to herself, she would also turn loneliness into companionship and sharing, once Francis could muster enough courage to give them up for her. If he gave Lady Poverty his need for love and companionship, she would give them back to him. Of that he was certain. It only remained for him to act on that conviction.

Meeting the Leper

Francis remembered the first victory of his new heart. All his life long he had panicked when he met a person with leprosy. And then one day on the road below Assisi, he did one of those surprising things that only the power of Jesus' Spirit could explain. He reached out and touched such a one, the very sight of whom nauseated him. He felt his knees playing tricks on him, and he was afraid he would not make it to the leper standing humbling before him. The odor of rotting flesh attacked all his senses as if he were smelling with his eyes and ears as well. Tears began to slide down his cheeks because he thought he wouldn't be able to do it; and as he began to lose his composure, he had to literally leap at the man before him. Trembling, he threw his arms around the leper's neck and kissed his cheek.

Then, like the feeling he remembered when he first began to walk, he was happy and confident; he stood erect and calm and loved this man in his arms. He wanted to hold him tighter but that would only be to satisfy himself now; and he was afraid to lose this newfound freedom. He dropped his arms and smiled, and the man's eyes twinkled back their recognition that Francis had received more than he had given. In the silence of their gazing, neither man dropped his eyes, and Francis marveled that a leper's eyes were hypnotically beautiful.

This New Day

This new day. This song for beginning again. This harmony within me. This weightlessness I feel.

Francis still caught glimpses from time to time of that first release, that beginning-anew feeling that filled his whole being the day he kissed the leper. The pent-up frustrations of his whole youth, the self-pity, the agonizing self-doubt and questioning, the moodiness of his illness—all rushed out of his heart as if a great dam had broken; and the backed-up, brackish waters of a lifetime streamed outdoors to be soaked up by the soil and forgotten forever.

That kiss, that reaching out of the lips directed his heart for the first time toward someone worth loving other than himself. He began that day to breathe out more than to breathe in, to turn outwards rather than inwards, to do rather than think about doing. He had finally found the courage to leap across that deep chasm that separated him from the other, from loving what he feared would demand more of him than he could give.

In keeping his eyes on the leper, in thinking only of this person before him, he forgot himself, he forgot the chasm beneath him, and he ran straight across the void into the arms of love and happiness. And all his life he struggled to preserve that original insight into love and to act it out daily. Love was looking into the eyes of the other; and forgetting the dark void between you and forgetting that no one can walk in a void, you start boldly across, your arms outstretched to give of yourself and to receive of the other.

In his last words to his brothers, his Testament, he said: "When I was in sin, it appeared too bitter to me to see lepers; and the Lord himself led me among them, and that which seemed bitter to me was changed for me into sweetness of soul and body." It was all there in those words: the walk to the leper was the Journey; what happened to you then was the Dream come true.

The Crucifix Speaks

He knew that a test was coming, an initiation into something he both feared and reverenced. That this new feeling would not last frightened him. In the past he had experienced so many ups and downs that he was suspicious of any new high. Still, there was a certainty about his Dreams that was more a conviction or a belief than a feeling or mood. As Francis mused on these thoughts, he approached the ramshackle little church of San Damiano. He hesitated a moment, then went in. Above the altar he saw the large Byzantine crucifix of Christ.

As though driven by an inner force, he fell on his knees and began to pray intensely. "Lord Jesus, what do you want me to do? Everyday I question my dream at Spoleto and wonder whether or not it was really you who spoke to me, or whether it was just my excitement about my coming baptism of fire as a Knight. Lord, my dreams plague me so. What do they mean? Why do I have such dreams and voices? What kind of man am I, Lord?"

Francis lifted his head from the stone floor and looked searchingly into the eyes of the crucifix that seemed now to have depth, like real eyes. Suddenly, the whole face of the Christ seemed to move, and Francis was afraid. Then as from some far-away place and yet coming surely from the crucifix, a voice clear and resonant pierced Francis' soul.

"Francis, go now and repair my church which, as you see, is falling down." Francis was jubilant. He waited for more, and he searched and searched the face of the crucifix, but there was no movement, no sign that more would come. Francis remained transfixed for a long time, and thanked Jesus over and over again for this clear request He had made of him. He would start rebuilding the church immediately.

It never occurred to Francis that Christ was asking anything other than the actual repairing of churches that were falling into ruin. So he ran from San Damiano and set about collecting stones to rebuild crumbling churches. He would start with San Damiano itself. His whole mind and energy were now focused almost fanatically on this one project.

This single-minded obedience to his dreams and voices was

to become a bold pattern in Francis' life that would lead to his total and radical service of the Gospel of Christ.

Losing a Father

Francis knew that the hardest test of all would be to stand up to his strong-willed father. They were two of a kind, in a way, each bent stubbornly upon what he thought mattered most in life. For Pietro it was power and influence and the satisfaction of accomplishment in the world of business and trade. For Francis it had become weakness and littleness and poverty of spirit that paradoxically gave him power and influence and satisfaction of spirit. If he could not meet his father face-to-face and stand up to him, he would erase everything that had happened in the cave.

His father had tried hard to cure Francis of his "silly notions" since his return from Spoleto; but when Francis sold some cloth and a horse and gave the money to the poor priest at San Damiano and then refused to come home, it was too much for Pietro. And the final insult came when Francis went begging through the streets of Assisi. He was shabby and unkempt and the crowds hissed and mocked that the son of the richest man in town should go begging for stones to repair churches.

One day when Francis was begging in the streets and the crowd was unusually loud in its abuse, he passed his father's shop. Pietro was livid with shame and heartbreak. He ran from the shop, collared Francis and dragged him before the Bishop of Assisi. It was then that Jesus gave Francis the courage to meet his father.

Calmly, Francis stripped himself of his clothes; and placing them reverently at the feet of his father, he declared in a strong voice, "I have called Pietro Bernardone my father....Now I will say Our Father who art in Heaven and not Pietro Bernardone." It was done, and Pietro realized he had gone too far with the boy. He wept inside for the son of his heart, but he would not make the first move toward reconciliation. What Francis had said was too final and too terrible to answer. The Bishop had covered Francis with his own cloak. And Francis left the court later that day clothed in a poor tunic that felt grander and more beautiful than all the finery in Assisi. The Dream had won.

An Emancipated Man

The winding, mountainous road to Gubbio! How dear the memories of his many trips to that little mountain town of St. Ubaldo, so like his own Assisi, so beloved because of his friend who had received him with love when he was no longer welcome in his father's house. It was in April of 1207 that he had abandoned his father, and leaving Assisi in a peasant's tunic, had set his face toward Gubbio.

That walk to Gubbio over the thickly wooded mountain to Valfabricca was to him like the first walk of Adam in the Garden of Paradise. The April sky was clear and the sun shone brightly; there still was snow in the mountain clefts and the air was crisp and invigorating. He felt completely free and all of nature seemed to belong to him once again, so different from that day after his long illness when he wandered about the hills of Assisi in his despondency.

Nature had now been transformed into a Paradise by his renunciation of all the security one normally would cling to. He had not anticipated this feeling of release, and so his own surprise enhanced his joy a hundredfold. And so full was this joy that he did what had become a habit for him in times of celebration; he broke out into song, a song of the Troubadours of Provencal.

Francis had just rounded the top of the mountain and was about to descend to Valfabricca when he heard a sudden rustling of leaves behind him. He whirled about still singing in full voice and stared into the eyes of a bandit chieftain. The man and the robber-band around him seemed more stunned than Francis himself. Then Francis startled them still further by singing aloud, "I am the Herald of the Great King!"

He chuckled every time he recalled the expressions on the bandits' faces. The leader shrugged his shoulders and his mustache, and pointing his forefinger toward his head, made little crazy-circles in the air. They all broke out laughing, including

Francis, whom they then seized and hurled into a deep cleft of snow. The robbers stood far above him still roaring with laughter and bowing and curtsying as they backed away waving their caps in the air. Francis, in the meantime, was having quite a time of it wiggling out of the snow, but he continued to sing and to enjoy the incident as much as apparently the robbers themselves did. Before long he was knocking the snow from his tunic and back on the trail through the mountains. His friend in Gubbio would be surprised to see him, and he had so much to tell him. If only he could communicate even a little of the complete emancipation of spirit that he was now experiencing. He hurried on to Gubbio for fear the feeling would pass before he had a chance to share it.

"Francesco? Francesco!"

His friend had seen him coming down the road and had recognized his walk but not his tunic.

"Francesco! What kind of costume is that supposed to be?"

"It is not a costume, Federico; it is my new life and my new freedom."

As they walked arm in arm back toward Federico's house, Francis told the story of all that had happened since those first days when Federico had accompanied him daily to the cave near Assisi and had waited for him outside while he prayed. And as he talked, water filled Federico's eyes, and Francis knew that he had understood.

His stay at his friend's house was very brief, for he wanted to live with the lepers in Gubbio. But Federico, in that one night that Francis spent with him, did something for which Francis would always be grateful: He gave Francis the hermit's tunic and cord and sandals which were to become the distinctive garb of the Lesser Brothers for all of Francis' earthly life and beyond it.

And Francis, clothed as a hermit of God, left Federico's house in the morning and went to live with the lepers of Gubbio, washing their sores and attending to their every need. Those were indeed idyllic days, and he always kept in his heart a special portion of affection for Federico and the little town of Gubbio, where he had tasted such sweetness of soul.

19

The Herald of a King

Faces in the crowd, always faces, staring at you or staring inward at themselves. Distracted faces, concentrated faces. Happy faces, anxious faces. Francis wanted to take them all to himself, to hold them between his hands and, looking quietly into their eyes, whisper, "Peace and good."

Some faces seemed to fix upon him the searching, expectant look of those whose journey had no end, of those who wandered aimlessly through life because they did not know what else to do, or because they were fleeing from something rather than toward something. For these Francis had the most compassion because they had no dream and because the dream would have to come from within themselves where all was barren desert. Or could someone else find the dream for them?

He began to wonder if everyone heard an inner Voice as he had, or whether some heard only human voices. If his Dream were something very special, then perhaps he would have to become a voice from Christ for others to hear. He would have to become the Herald of Christ, singing aloud the glory of the Dream that God had made for everyone. As he walked about the countrysides and through the streets of all the world, he would imagine that he was taking each face from the anonymous crowds and breathing hope and love into it. He would share the Dream.

So, in sackcloth robe and with a poor rope tightened around his waist and a cross chalked on the front and back, Francis set out like a knight clad in the finest armor and bearing the shield of the King of Kings. In his excitement and joy, he cried aloud, "I am the Herald of the Great King." It mattered nothing to him that a herald was never a knight, and a knight never a herald.

He smiled now with tears in his eyes as he thought of what a fool he must have seemed to anyone who heard him crying aloud, "I am the Herald of the Great King," and then saw him skipping along the road, a poor little wisp of a man, the very picture of a Court Fool. How lovely it all was, and even now in memory he felt stronger, and almost tried to rise from the ground and set out again, the King-Fool-Herald-Lover of the Word.

The Fool

It seemed to Francis, once Jesus had taken his heart, that one word summed up everything, and that word was "trust." Jesus trusted him to become perfect as his heavenly Father was perfect. He knew something of trust from working in his father's shop. People would come in and buy an expensive bolt of cloth, pay for it, and ask him to put it under the shelf until later that day. They trusted him to recognize them and to give them the cloth without any difficulties. That was a certain kind of trust, surely, a trust in his honesty and his memory.

But this new trust that Jesus had placed in him was much bigger in its implications. God's own Son had spoken to him, had asked him to rebuild his church. He understood now that request meant more than brick and mortar. It meant that he, Francis, was to re-create in his own person the life of Jesus on earth. He was to be obedient to God's Word, chaste in mind and heart, poor in everything. How that was to rebuild God's Church he did not know, but he suspected that it would follow, as his father Pietro always said, from being a good steward. As a good shopkeeper, Pietro was confident that all other shopkeepers would eventually have to follow his example to survive the competition. If Francis were holy and Christlike, those who saw him would eventually look at their own following of Christ in view of what Francis himself was.

And that was what scared him. He did not want people to compare themselves to him, but to Christ. Would he become proud of being a holy man? Perhaps. But that was the gamble he would have to take. Jesus had placed His trust in him, and for His own reasons, expected this poor young son of a shopkeeper to be His intimate friend and confidant. It was like all friendship, Francis thought; you don't anticipate it, and when it happens, you kill it by analyzing it too much. Friendship, God's especially, is a gift. You receive it reverently and gratefully, and you hope you measure up to this person's trust in opening up to you, in having the courage to reach across the chasm of uncertainty to you, believing that, yes, you will say, I like you, too. Of course, Jesus must have known he would say yes, but Francis still thought it all so wonderful! Even into this poor, proud little town of Assisi

God's love reached down and filtered through the narrow street until it surprised you coming around a corner unawares, lost in your own selfish thoughts.

Thoughts! How they had changed. Now he was almost always distracted, lost somewhere in Jesus. It must be affecting his manner, too, because when he did notice someone looking at him, it was with a strange smile, almost a smirk that said, "Poor Francis, surely he has become mad. A fool maybe, maybe a poet, but surely mad." Then Francis would smile and say, "Peace and good," and he wondered if that sounded funny, too. Everything, since his conversion, seemed to come out funny, even a bit insincere-sounding. He didn't know why. Maybe it was because people just don't do that sort of thing, going around praising Jesus and smiling and loving with their eyes.

Francis loved everyone with his eyes. Did they see it? He hoped that they would. And what if their eyes loved back, too, eventually? That would be lovely and would make being considered crazy seem like so small a price to pay.

That thought made Francis so happy that he ran out into the street, bounded up the steep steps to the church of San Rufino, sat down at the door and greeted everyone who entered with a, "Peace and good." Most people he noticed, were annoyed; others thought him a harmless madman and smiled condescendingly at him, and a few gave him a knowing wink, which said, "Stick it out, Francis; we'll come round eventually in our own good time." He was happy for the winkers.

A Wind in Your Face

The joy of tramping the roads in spring, the wind blowing in your face, and the larks showing off overhead. Francis always felt like running and shouting on a warm day in spring, especially if he had just come from the mountain where it was perpetually cold and wet. Having the road all to yourself was part of the fun of being free, part of the reward for the heartache of separation from the comfortable society you had left behind. You hadn't a care in the world and nature was a garden just for you to romp in.

To Francis everything in him and around him was a gift from his Father in Heaven. He expected nothing, so he was grateful for everything. Even a piece of earth was cause for rejoicing, and he thanked God always for everything that was. He held everything to his heart with the enthusiasm of a child surprised by some unexpected toy. The air he breathed, the sounds he heard, the sights and smells of all the world entered his grateful soul through senses perfected by gratitude and purity of heart. Nothing was evil, for everything came from God, and evil came only from a heart that chose not to love. The heart through passion or selfishness or pride could choose not to love and that was evil, but no thing or no person was evil in and of itself.

When Francis passed people on the road or met them on their doorsteps as he begged, he could not hide his delight in them, in their very existence. All people to Francis were good gifts to brighten his day with the mystery of their unique personalities. As he ran along the roads of Umbria in spring, he wanted to shout to everyone he met how glorious it was to be alive, how beautiful it was in the garden God had made. He wanted to tell the trees and flowers, the animals and birds, the streams and rivers, the hills and plains how wonderful they were, and how much joy to human beings and praise to God they gave, just by being there and celebrating themselves.

And he was not worried or anxious about yesterday, today, or tomorrow because Christ is, and all things are in Him and He is in the Father. Francis no longer worried, not because he was a naive optimist, but because he had become in prayer and penance a realist who saw the unimportance of everything but God, and in God and with God and through God, the importance of everything. God was everywhere; the divine presence charged creation with a power and glory that made everything shine with beauty and goodness in Francis' eyes. God's touch on everything inspirited everything that was.

Francis wanted more than anything else to leave behind in everyone an attitude of celebration. Union with God, with every man, with every woman, with every child, with every thing was love, and love brought joy, not gloom. When religion was gloom, then the heart had gone out of it and Christ's warning against pharisaical observance had been forgotten.

True worship, true celebration in Francis' mind was like

tramping the roads in spring, the wind blowing in your face and the larks showing off overhead. And you lifted your arms and heart to God and shouted, "Amen," even when a thunderstorm was mounting above you.

The Troubadour

Francis loved to sing. It freed his spirit and turned the human voice, so often an organ of selfishness and sin, into an instrument of celebration. How he had thrilled to the songs of the French Troubadours who traveled down into Italy from southern France. Bernard of Ventadour, Pierre Vidal, Peirol of Auvergne. Every time one of these great singers came through Assisi, Francis would be imitating him for months afterwards, entertaining his friends and delighting in their praise of his beautiful young voice.

Francis so loved this performing that once, before his conversion, he went so far as to have a Troubadour's costume tailored just for him. And he cut a pretty dashing figure, too, for the slight man that he was. He would start walking and acting like a minstrel the minute he put on his parti-colored hose and pointed shoes, the hooded tunic with the lute slung behind. He reflected now how much his dress had always affected his behavior. There was something in the simple tunic he put on that day he left his father that altered his whole bearing, from an important, vain Troubadour of Assisi to a poor little insignificant singer.

But his voice did not deteriorate. In fact, it sounded more beautiful to Francis, because now he was not trying to impress anybody. He was simply giving voice to the joy within him and to the beauty he saw all around him. Whenever he felt his heart constricting again, he would break into a song of joy and praise. Or he would remember a song of the Troubadours whose words he never had to change, so perfectly did they fit his Lady Poverty. There was one by Arnaut Daniel that he specially loved:

> Softly sighs the April air
> Before the coming of May.

24

Joy is everywhere
When the first leaf sees the day.
And shall I alone despair
Turning from sweet love away?
Something to my heart replies,
You too were for rapture strung.
Why else the dreams that rise
Round you when the year is young?

Yes, a thousand times, yes! Francis loved that image of himself as a lute strung for rapture. He wanted to stand in the wind of April afternoons and let the Holy Spirit play upon him for all the world to hear the beauty of his music. And in every season he tried to be strung and tuned for the hand of Jesus to play upon His poor little instrument, made perfect and resonant by the skill of Jesus Himself.

Francis' Mystical Marriage

To speak of love had never been difficult for Francis until Christ stole his heart. Then there was something so sacred about their relationship that all love became love caught up in Jesus.

When he heard the Gospel read at Mass, it was Jesus speaking directly to him, and every word was a love-word. He swallowed each word and assimilated it into his whole being. He wanted to become one with the Word, to make literally his own the Word of God. This Word of God was its own message, because Jesus was the Word and by becoming a man he had put flesh onto His own message of love. He *was* the Word. So when Francis heard the Gospels read aloud, it was as if Jesus Himself were entering his ears and filling his whole self with His presence. And the word he listened to took on flesh in Francis himself.

The demands of Jesus were hard, but to Francis they were love-requests and the harder they seemed, the more elated he was that Jesus should ask him. It was a privilege far surpassing any gift that earthly lovers gave one another. And Francis basked in the sunlight and pleasure of Jesus' company. Had the Lord asked nothing of him, he would have felt small and neglected like a knight who is not trusted with great feats but must be satisfied with helping orphans and widows while the great knights were away fighting huge battles to secure good in the land. He knew Jesus loved him because He made such terrible demands of him, the most difficult of which were the invitations all through the Gospels to leave everyone and everything for His sake. But the more Francis renounced, the more he possessed, pressed down and flowing over. It seemed that Jesus wanted Francis to give up everything so that He could have the joy of returning it as a gift to Francis. That way Jesus could keep handing back what Francis had first given Him, and there would be an eternal effort to outdo one another in selflessness. They understood each other and were becoming one flesh in a manner that man and woman could never duplicate. And that was love as Francis had hoped it would be.

So celibacy for Francis was not something sterile and barren, and he never thought of celibacy anyway, but of virginity, which was more positive and implied something you choose for the Kingdom rather than something you endure because of your role in the Church. Virginity brought fullness to Francis because, in renouncing marriage, he did not shrink as a person but grew in his capacity to love more and more people. He moved in a world much larger than the family.

Besides, his identification with Jesus was so absolute and literal that he could never be anything other than a virgin like Christ. Francis thought that Jesus' own virginity made possible His total love for him, and vice versa. And the paradox in Francis' life was that his exclusive love for Jesus was at the same time inclusive of all humanity. Again what he had renounced had come rushing down in waterfalls of new capacities for love and giving. And the pool of self was constantly refilled with the fresh and clean water of love that flowed out of Francis in countless streams of attention, affection and service of others. The living waters of Jesus had become his own, and he thereby became a reservoir of unselfish love for all creatures.

The Demon and the Angel

And then the temptations! How they had plagued him at first when he was alone and the pull of his former home was so strong upon his heart, drawing him back to the security of Assisi. But he somehow remained on the plain below the city, caring for the lepers and waiting for Jesus to drive away the demon in his heart. The greatest temptation was to feel sorry for himself and to ask himself why no one really cared what he was doing. Yes, the lepers were grateful. That he knew, but he could not expect from the poor people the companionship he needed to sustain him in his service of them.

So Francis lived in prayer. He cast himself totally upon Jesus and begged Him to let one poor man survive this test of selflessness. In his daily washing of the lepers' sores Francis learned that love was hard, not soft and sentimental as he had guessed it would be. Every day he had to remind himself that he must discipline his own feelings if he was to become God's instrument. Love itself, he slowly grew to understand, could be the demon in his heart, if by love one understood a sweet consoling feeling that ran over at the heart and made a little puddle of piety in the soul. And that kind of demon was hardest to root out because it looked and felt so much like real love.

But when life became difficult and lonely and there was no return for giving of yourself, then this demon-love showed itself for what it really was, and you turned away from the path and abandoned the Quest. Jesus had said, "No one putting a hand to the plow and looking back is fit for the Kingdom of Heaven." Francis believed that to the end, for he knew what would have happened had he looked back during those first months when he was all alone in his service of the lepers in the little colony below Assisi. There is no prettier sight in Italy than the one from that spot: the pink and brown buildings of Assisi huddled close together on a green buttress of Mount Subasio, the very picture of warmth and security.

But Jesus knew what Francis' heart could take, and He sent him His angel to comfort him and lift his heart again. That angel, as so often was the case in his life, was a person, the first brother to join Francis in the Journey. His name was Bernard of

Quintavalle, and he, like Francis, never looked back from the Quest he had begun.

The Brothers

When Bernard of Quintavalle and the others came to him, Francis rejoiced that his journey had not ended once the Spirit took over his life, but that a new and more exciting Journey had begun, a journey even now only beginning.

Brother Bernard was, in Francis' eyes, the real founder of the Order of Lesser Brothers, because he was the first wealthy Assisian to sell all his possessions, give them to the poor, and throw himself completely upon the mercy of God. Francis remembered so vividly the night he spent in the home of the wealthy merchant, Bernard of Quintavalle. Bernard, pretending to be asleep, had spent the night watching Francis at prayer, and in the morning had told Francis of his resolve to renounce his possessions and to follow Francis in the footsteps of Christ.

Francis was utterly stunned. Never, in his wildest hopes, had he imagined that God would so quickly answer his prayers for companionship in poverty and pursuit of the Dream. But he did not immediately show his joy and relief to Bernard. Instead, Francis said that they must go together to the bishop's house where there was a poor priest who would say Mass for them. Afterwards they would ask the priest to open the Book of the Gospels three times to see what God would there reveal to them about their future; whether Bernard was to follow Christ as Francis' brother, or not.

Francis' heart always beat faster when he recalled those three openings of the Gospels:

"If you wish to be perfect, go and sell all your possessions, and give to the poor...and come, follow me."

"Take nothing for your journey, neither staff nor knapsack, shoes nor money."

"Anyone who will come after me must renounce self, take up the cross and follow me."

With the words "nothing for your Journey" still clanging

in his ears, Francis threw his arms around Bernard's neck and kissed his cheeks. And Bernard went out and sold all his goods and gave the money to the poor. And Francis and Bernard kept the Dream warm together as they journeyed side by side across the hills and plains of Umbria.

Of Intimacy

Now, with his head resting on Brother Masseo's shoulder, Francis remembered the corner of the piazza and the girl with the sad eyes. He had left the piazza convinced that loneliness was the price to be paid for the Dream. Yet from the moment in Bishop Guido's Palace when he renounced his father, he had never actually been lonely. Nor, after the brothers began to come, was he ever really alone. In fact many times he had yearned for solitude, to be alone with the Dream. Yet when he did escape to the mountains, he would always return again to his brothers. He needed them. They were Christ's gift to him because Jesus understood him and his moods, his need for the physical presence of others to help keep the Dream a dream.

Brother Masseo, especially, was for Francis the warmth and goodness that soothed his spirit when the fear was upon him. He always thought of it as "the fear," because he did not understand it, and when it came, it was without warning and for no apparent reason. It was like the ghost of his long illness as a young man coming back to haunt him, to scare him into despair again. Francis recalled with a shudder how often this fear came during the first months after his conversion, before Bernard of Quintavalle joined him. Bernard broke the spell of the fear, or at least its frequency.

But it was Masseo who killed the fear. When Masseo came, he was like St. George, a handsome giant of a man hovering about Francis, slaying his demons. The first time Francis noticed this quality in Masseo was one winter's day when they were on the road returning from a begging tour through the streets of Assisi. The housewives had naturally given better portions of food to the gallant Masseo, who was tall and handsome and who made the slight Francis look poor and unmeritable in comparison. Francis rejoiced at this and his heart was skipping for joy as they trudged through the mud on their way to Saint Mary of the Angels.

Suddenly, as they rounded a little hill, they met one of his father's pack trains returning from France loaded with new cloth for the coming spring bazaar. Without warning the fear gripped him and he went empty and cold inside. He tried not to show it, but the feeling was too strong and he ran wildly into the woods. Masseo, stunned at his behavior and thinking it was another of Francis' pranks, followed close at his heels. They beat down the branches of underbrush and charged straight into the thickest part of the wood.

On some crazy impulse Masseo suddenly reached out and tripped Francis, and they tumbled into the mud and began to wrestle. He pinned Francis to the ground and then jumped away in fear when he saw Francis' face beneath him. Francis was trembling and tears were running from his eyes. Masseo was dumbfounded. He did what only Masseo, of all the brothers, would have done. He bent over and took Francis in his arms and carried him to a large dry rock and silently set him down. Then he sat down beside Francis and put his arm around his shoulders and started to sing a little Provencal lullaby. Francis leaned his head on Masseo's shoulder and he did not dissolve and the Dream shone brightly in his heart and the demon dissolved.

Of Wholeness and Sincerity

Walking through the narrow streets in the spring rain of Assisi afternoons, Francis found great peace. Everyone was at siesta and the streets were abandoned by every living thing. Then the town was his, and he would play hide-and-seek with Masseo and Leo through the maze of streets and alleyways, or else he would walk alone in the rain. Then at times, with the rain washing the pink stone clean and with freshness everywhere, he would look longingly at his father's house where he knew they were warm within and the cooking meats and good wine floated sweet rich aromas through the great halls. And he would look down at his bare feet and ragged tunic and wonder.

But always the rain would stop and people would throw open their shutters and pour into the streets again. And Francis would see in their eyes that he had chosen the better part. They should have walked in the rain like him to wash the fear and tiredness from their eyes. The steady shifting of the eyes among the wealthiest patrons of the town made Francis' heart go heavy, and he wanted so much to free them from the great weight of their seriousness about their own money and property. But most of the time they would not even look him in the eye.

Francis had noticed from the beginning that when he went begging, especially, very few people looked into his eyes. They seemed always to avoid eye contact, either from embarrassment or fear or contempt. There were, of course, the few bright-eyed, open people whose eyes were surely the lamps of their whole selves radiating love and goodness and trust.

It was marvelous how people became who they really were once you reached out your hand to them in the gesture of the beggar. Even the insight into people he had gained in his father's shop paled when compared to what he learned begging in the streets of Assisi. So often the veneer of respectability would be sloughed off and something like a monster would emerge, cursing and destroying you with the venom of words and gestures. It was an experience only beggars understood.

From these harrowing experiences Francis determined to be always on the outside what he was on the inside. He knew that some of the brothers felt he overdid this obsession with sincerity and wholeness, but Francis feared duplicity and hypocrisy more than anything in all the world. It was against hypocrisy that Jesus had railed again and again in the Gospels, and Francis was sure Jesus would never speak harshly against anything unless it spoiled the human heart and made the Holy Spirit's entry there impossible.

Once when he was ill, a doctor had insisted that he wear some warm patches of cloth next to his skin. Francis had agreed to do so only if soft patches were sewn to the outside of his tunic as well. Otherwise people might think that he had on only the coarse tunic of penance when in reality it was padded inside with soft, warm garments. Francis had discarded the soft patches as soon as he was better, for the Gospel of Jesus told him those who

wear soft garments live in the palaces of kings.
And Francis would never again live in a palace, or even in
a house. He was a street person, a man of the road who bore his
palace with him in his own heart. He had taken up residence
within himself and had become a portable kingdom moving along
the streets and roads of the world. Jesus had said, "The Kingdom
of Heaven is within you." What need was there of palaces built
of stone? And if he remained sincere in poverty and whole in his
freedom from material things, who knows how many would take
to the roads in countless movable courts of love?

Of War

Glancing over his shoulder as he left the piazza, Francis noticed
a knight sitting on a great charger and talking to a young boy
who was obviously in awe of the gallant man in his polished
armor and doublet of deep scarlet. All the memories rushed in.
He saw himself in the little open-mouthed boy, and he
remembered his fascination at the knights who rode into the
piazzas of Assisi with the clatter of horse and the ring of metal
clacking in the air. He would rush from his father's shop and up
the little incline to the Piazza Commune and stand staring in
wonder at so glorious a sight.

The knight represented everything he had wanted to
become. Courageous, yet courteous and kind; a feared foe in the
field and yet a genteel protector of the weak and helpless; fierce
in the face of evil, yet gentle and handsome before the ladies. And
then he had gone to war in one of the countless skirmishes
between Assisi and Perugia, the powerful neighbor to the north.
He rode out of Assisi with the seriousness of Charlemagne
himself, and he could see out of the corner of his fixed, determined
eyes that the young boys of Assisi flushed with pride as he passed.

But all that pomp and ceremony was dashed to the ground
at Ponte San Giovanni where the army of Assisi was defeated and
Francis himself taken prisoner. There at the bridge halfway
between Assisi and Perugia he saw for the first time the real face
of war, and it was ugly and plain, and there was no glory in it,

even for the victor. And yet, so strong was the call of chivalry and honor that after a year's imprisonment in Perugia and a long illness at home, he set out again with the forces of Walter of Brienne. He did not, however, have to see the squalor of war once again because at Spoleto, only a short ride from Assisi, he had the Vision, the Dream that changed his life. And all his life from that moment on, his heart was turned away from making war to making peace.

The same virtues were there: courage and courtesy, chivalry and adventure, honor and fierceness of purpose. But now it was not in war that they were tested but in the battle inside the human heart. Francis saw that the real battle was inside, and if that battle could be won, the call to arms would no longer be necessary. He did not know if that was possible; he only tried to make it come true in his own heart and hope that others would follow his example.

He had begun to think small instead of big, to start with himself instead of with forces and people outside. And he prayed that someday that little boy in the piazza would stand open-mouthed and flushed with excitement to see a barefoot beggar walk across the square with eyes that flashed with victory and ragged clothes that shone with the radiance of purity and poverty of spirit.

Rivotorto

Francis always thought of the early days of the brotherhood as the Rivotorto times. In those days the brothers all huddled together in a single sty through the heat of summer into the cold and wet autumn of winter's chills and into spring when the rains kept floors and walls constantly damp, and the whole interior was musty. Those were the happy times. It was so crowded in the shelter that Francis had to chalk little boundaries on the ceiling. The brothers would then sleep beneath their own chalkmark, approximately, because some were fat and some skinny, some tall and others short. No one minded then and any of them would have been glad to sleep outside in the snow, so great was their love for the poor Jesus of Nazareth.

That was the honeymoon of their marriage to Lady Poverty, and the brotherhood never again captured the rapture of those days. Francis never thought of Rivotorto, as that place was called, without weeping. No lovers had ever had so glorious a honeymoon as he and his brothers had there in that pigsty at the bend of the river beneath the Umbrian sky.

They all realized that honeymoons don't last forever, but they kept hoping that maybe this one would. It did not. As more and more brothers came into the fraternity, the simplicity of Rivotorto died and a more rigid structure was born. And when this complexity entered into the idyllic days of the woods and fields, Francis knew he must go to the Pope for his wisdom and guidance on what the brothers should do.

It was not that he felt the need for some structure for this new community of men who were forming around him, but Francis did want some kind of official sanction for his way of life in poverty and some ecclesiastical protection for his brothers. There were bands of reformers and fanatics roaming the countryside at the time who were leading the common folk down blind alleys of heretical enthusiasm. Francis wanted to know that he was not himself one of these weird itinerant preachers whose preaching was more self-serving than inspired. And the only source of certainty for *him* was the Church of Christ as personified in the pope.

Francis felt for the Pope a reverence and awe that went beyond the fear some people of his time had for the papal power and influence. Francis saw in the Pope the tangible representative of Jesus. He believed that the Pope was the personal link between Christ and humanity. For him the papal word of approval would be Christ's own approval of Francis' interpretation of the Gospel.

He would go now to Rome, down the valley through the Umbrian countryside to the city of Peter. In Rome sat Innocent III, the shrewd leader of the Church of God. Francis understood, as every Christian of his time did, that no matter how clear the voice of God sounded within you, there was no assurance that it was in fact God's voice unless the Church gave approval. The Roman Court was the discerner of spirits for every Christian of the 13th century.

So Francis and a few of the brothers set out from Rivotorto on the long walk to Rome.

The Pope and the Beggar

It is one of the wonders of life that we meet souls compatible with our own in places and circumstances unexpected and surprising. This fact never so thoroughly overwhelmed Francis as in his audience with Pope Innocent III. This magnificent man had Francis' own suspicions and mistrust of anything that smacked of fanaticism, and in Francis' first meeting with the Pope, he had sensed the Pope's mind working intensely behind the fixed and penetrating gaze. His eyes were like shafts of light illuminating the dark corners of Francis' soul. And when the audience was over, Francis had no idea what the Pope really felt. Everything was in abeyance.

That night, as Innocent later related to Francis, the Pope dreamed that the Church of St. John Lateran, the mother church of Christendom, began to lean on its side and topple to the ground. Then, just as the nightmare was pounding most loudly in the Pope's brain and the church was crashing to the ground, a little beggar leaped from the shadows and supported the falling building on his own shoulders. The Pope, waking with a shudder of relief, recognized the beggar as Francis, the poor man from Assisi.

Now Innocent never put much stock in nightmares, but there was about this dream the power and persuasion of a vision, and he resummoned Francis and the brothers the following day. It was at this audience that Francis saw in Pope Innocent a heart like his own. The Pope's whole personality radiated the intensity and seriousness of a child. And unlike most other people to whom Francis had stretched out his hands in supplication, this man looked straight into his eyes. Francis would never forget their complete candor and innocence. How fitting the name Innocent!

As Francis slowly and deliberately explained the Dream, the Pope's eyes grew moist, and he loved Francis with his eyes. At that moment Francis knew that the Dream was from God and that this soft man with the hard exterior would stand by the Dream and write it down in the Book of the Visions of the Church of God.

Innocent in fact did more. He rose from his throne and embraced Francis, and Francis felt through the rich papal garments the beating of a poor and ragged heart like his own, who longed to change places with any one of these beggars and fools of Christ. Francis wept aloud, not only for joy that the Dream was real, but because the touch of this man was the softness he had always longed for from his own father. The Pope had become more than the tangible representative of Christ. He was the father he had lost, given back a hundredfold. In their embrace Francis felt that he in turn was for Innocent the son he had given up for Christ, returned again a hundredfold.

The Cardinals, meanwhile, looked on in astonishment at the tender scene being enacted shamelessly in full view of the whole Papal Court. Some of them grumbled at the melodrama of it all, but others, their eyes moist as well, understood.

Then Pope Innocent simply and humbly proclaimed for all to hear, "Go with God, little brothers, and announce salvation for all, as the Lord reveals it to you! And when the Almighty has multiplied your number, then come back to me and I will charge you with a greater inheritance."

A greater inheritance! What he had felt in the Pope's embrace was true: Francis had been restored to his father's house, and a new and spiritual inheritance was his. From that day on the bond between Francis and Innocent was ever that of son and father, and Francis always included Pope Innocent among the Lesser Brothers of Jesus.

Of Lady Clare

One scene Francis always held dearly in his memory was the astonished look on the faces of the townspeople that day in the Bishop's Palace when he laid his clothes at the feet of his Father, and Bishop Guido covered his nakedness with his own cloak. One face in particular always stood out because of its intensity and the compassion in the eyes. It was the beautiful face of Clare, the daughter of Favarone, a nobleman of Assisi. She must have been 13 or 14 at the time, and she stood peeking out between two matrons in open-eyed wonder at so strange a thing as Francis had just done.

As he stood there secure in the Bishop's embrace, he smiled at this young girl with the long fair hair whose reputation was impeccable even among the coarsest of his former companions. Three years later, at the sweetest time of adolescence, she was to come to him and beg to follow him in perfect poverty of life. He would never forget the look on her face—the wrinkled brow and the fierce eyes.

The terrible seriousness of her young resolve almost made him laugh at the time, for she was so young and so stubbornly noble. He was glad now he hadn't laughed, for Clare never swerved from her determination to keep intact the ideals that Jesus had whispered into Francis' ear. Never for one second was the Lady Clare a disappointment to him as his own brothers had been time and again.

He recalled tenderly her words of profession before the altar of St. Mary of the Angels: "I want only Jesus Christ, and to live by the Gospel, owning nothing, and in chastity." The brothers' hearts were warmed by the unction of her words and by the sight of Francis, snipping off her soft hair and handing her the rough habit of poverty with its white veil of chastity. He then led her out of St. Mary of the Angels to the Benedictine Convent at Bastia. It was the proudest walk in his life, for he knew he was presenting to Christ Jesus a bride who was the envy of every woman in Assisi, and a woman whose capacity for love had not even begun to be tested.

Later on good Bishop Guido gave Francis the church at San Damiano to be the home of Clare and her sisters, and Francis had wept tears of joy, for this was the church that Francis himself had restored. He had taken literally the voice of the crucifix in San Damiano, "Francis, go and repair my church." And now that church and that crucifix were in the constant care of that extraordinary woman, Clare. Perhaps he had not been wrong in taking his Lord's words literally to heart, for in his simplicity he had prepared a fitting home for Christ's own brides.

Francis smiled at the irony of it, and he was enough of a poet to realize that everything symbolic must begin with the literal. At San Damiano's the symbolic and literal were one. He had restored this church and this church would restore the world.

A Radical Man

In the long days and longer nights before the Dream came true, Francis wondered if the Journey he had set upon would really bring him to his destination. When he was a boy, every trip he took out beyond the walls of Assisi brought him to some place where he could say, "I'm here in this place; I have arrived." But this Journey was different. It pointed to the very roots of Christ's own life. Its end was somewhere in the real meaning of Jesus' words. It was a trip backwards to the literal Gospel life and forward into the Kingdom and inward to the heart where dwelled the Trinity. And you could never say, "I have arrived."

It was a Journey of decisions as radical as the Gospel itself. At every fork in the road, there was a narrow, difficult way and a wide, easy way to travel. And Francis was continually surprised with the paradoxical joy that the harder road would bring, time after time. Still, at every road the easier way attracted him with almost hypnotic persuasion.

He never took the easy roads, not because he wanted to punish himself or the brothers, but because that is the way he read the Gospel. If Christ's words meant something else, then he was too ignorant to understand what that deeper, more hidden meaning was. He looked upon himself as a simple man from Umbria who expected words to mean what they said. That was all he was capable of.

And once he heard and understood the Word of God, he tried to put it into practice in his own life. For him the Word was life and not to live it was to deprive oneself of really living. That was what the Dream was all about in his own mind: to dare to live radically and simply, to take a chance on Christ. And what caused inestimable joy in Francis and his brothers was that the Gospel worked. If you tried to live it without reservation, you suddenly experienced a whole new worldview, and you felt as though you had never lived before. Living became so precious that every moment was delicious and filled with the danger of risk and challenge, and the meaning of love came clear. Francis could never be grateful enough for the Dream. It enabled him to embrace life and love, suffering and doubt as one. He and the brothers became living, tangible symbols that life could be lived, and no thinking person could be indifferent to the Lesser Brothers. Their challenge to the values of their times was unmistakable. It was a challenge as hard as the rock of the caves they lived in and as gentle as the love they bore each other.

Francis sent the brothers out as living challenges to complacency and smugness. He hoped that everyone who saw them would wonder, "What should be my response to these fools? They are mad, but would that I were, too. The only think I lack is the courage to be carefree and mad like these beggars from Assisi." And Francis prayed day and night that God would give all people the courage to be themselves instead of what others expected them to be.

He did not want everyone to enter the brotherhood or to join the Lady Clare and her sisters. He only wanted people to be free, to be what they wanted to be in their own hearts. For God spoke differently to each person, calling one to marriage, another to virginity; one to the city, another to the country; one to work with the mind, another with the hands. But who was brave enough to look inside and ask: "Is this what I should be doing, what I really want to do with my life?"

The Lady Clare left nobility to become a beggar, but his brother Pope Innocent remained Vicar of Christ's Church. And both were totally free, really doing what they had *decided* they should do. Both were living their own lives and not someone else's. Who could do more?

Of Brotherly Love

In these dying days of his life in the body when Francis thought of his brothers, his greatest concern was that they remain a brotherhood. He feared, from what he had seen in some of the earlier monasteries, that they would become men who live together and take their meals together but rarely care about each other in that intimate way that he and his first companions had served one another and loved one another, "washing each other's feet." Francis believed with all his heart that if the brothers really loved one another, then they would always remain in the brotherhood, knowing that nowhere else was God so close than when brothers loved one another sincerely and without shame.

And when they traveled afar, they would always seek out the brothers of their Order, knowing that they were one family and that they belonged together. He used to admonish his brothers with these words, "Brothers, if a mother loves and cherishes her own child in the flesh, how much more should we love and cherish our brothers in the spirit." And Francis had meant quite literally what he said: The brothers' devotion to one another should exceed that of a mother for her child.

He knew he was asking the heroic, but that was what the Dream was all about. The pursuit of the ideal of Poverty was possible only if there was love. Without love, the Quest became a journey of pride and empty idealism. Of course, it worked the other way, too. Should the brothers abandon the Dream of Gospel Poverty, then love, for them, became a kind of selfishness and their living together would degenerate into convenience and ease and comfort.

Francis smiled at the complexity of his own thoughts. Brother Elias would surely frown at such complicated thinking from someone so simple as Francis. But Brother Leo, who had copied down his words and listened to his thoughts, would not frown, nor would he smile. Brother Leo always understood the difference between being simple and being a simpleton. One is not born simple; one becomes simple by walking the maze-like journey out of the cavern of self into the light. The soul is complex and God is simple and the closer one approaches God, the simpler one becomes in Faith and Hope and Love. To be completely simple is to be God, and Francis knew how far he was from being God. His constant prayer was, "Who are You, O God, and what am I?" Brother Leo had told him there was no more profound and complicated question in all the world. A simpleton could ask the question, but only one who is simple could grasp how complicated and rich those simple words were.

Francis prayed them again now, changing them just a bit. "Who are You, O God, and what are we, Your poor little brothers of the Dream?" He hoped his brothers would always be simple, be whole enough, to see how interconnected and complex those words were. God, Brothers, the Dream. They were a trinity, and the Journey held them together in a simple, indivisible unity.

Hot Porridge and Holiness

One thing puzzled Francis all his life long, and that was the seemingly great happiness of some publicly known sinners and the gloom that seemed to veil the faces of so many pious souls. There were men and women he knew in Assisi, who lived with an exuberance and carefree spirit that radiated enthusiasm for life, and they "sinned" with great exhilaration and abandon, never seeming to regret anything of the past and embracing the present with joy. Francis never believed they were the sinners that people thought they were, and he was instinctively drawn to these simple celebrators of life. He could understand why Jesus had associated with sinners and publicans if they were anything like these men and women of Assisi. They were often more honest and more basically good than some pious souls he knew. Perhaps there was a great chasm between piety and goodness. Piety, after all, was something mainly external and goodness was in the heart. Perhaps, too, joy and enthusiasm for life, like charity, absolved a multitude of sins.

He saw the distinction between piety and goodness manifested quite clearly in his brothers. The holiest of them were anything but pious. They joked and laughed and took life much less seriously than saints were supposed to. And Francis loved them for it. They saved the brotherhood from those melancholy personalities whose goodness he never questioned, but whose gloom cast a pall over some of the communities of brothers.

If only all the brothers could have a touch of Brother Juniper, the little clown of God. He was a perpetual tonic for Francis, especially during trying times or when he was beginning to take himself too seriously. Brother Juniper was entirely what Francis ever strove to be, a living symbol of the joy of loving God.

Nor was Juniper so naive as some thought him to be. True, he was guileless, but because of that he often could correct the brothers better than anyone else, for no one took offense at what he said. And correct them he did! Francis remembered one story very clearly, even though it was only repeated to him, and he did not actually witness the incident himself.

Brother Juniper had been staying with some brothers whose Brother Guardian was quite a stern though competent and practical superior. Juniper had that afternoon—during siesta yet—given a lavish alms to a beggar who appeared at the door of their hut. The good Guardian reprimanded Brother Juniper for being so prodigal with the goods that had been begged with so much humility by this poor community of brothers.

In the middle of the night the Brother Guardian felt a tugging at his tunic; and when he opened his bleary eyes, there was Brother Juniper beaming from ear to ear and offering the Guardian a big bowl of boiling porridge. The Brother Guardian was furious; but before he could utter a word, Juniper announced disarmingly, "Brother Guardian, I noticed that when you reprimanded me this afternoon, your voice was a bit hoarse. This porridge with this huge lump of butter I put into it will do wonders for your throat and chest." The guardian, who was anything but stupid, understood immediately what Juniper was doing, and he dismissed both him and the porridge as sternly as he could.

Juniper, a good match for this man, was not one to be put off that easily, so he said to the still drowsy but angry Guardian, "Well, Brother Guardian, if you won't eat this porridge, we certainly mustn't let it go to waste in a community as poor as this one! Would you mind very much holding this bowl, so *I* can eat the porridge?"

And with that Brother Juniper thrust the hot bowl into the fumbling hands of the startled Guardian and began to eat with

enormous enthusiasm and noise. The Brother Guardian was so taken aback that he burst out laughing at the ludicrous position he had let himself get into. The two men ended up eating the porridge together and swapping stories about how serious some of the brothers were becoming.

Of all the stories of the brothers, Francis delighted most in that one. He would tell the story to the new brothers and then say, "Oh, if only we had a whole grove of junipers like this one!" And with that Francis would gather up his tunic and begin running through the woods screaming and hollering, jumping up and clicking his bare heels together while the poor novices stood open-mouthed and shocked at this silly performance from the "great" Father Francis, who had inspired them by his littleness and fervor of soul to leave everything and follow the poor Christ of the Gospels. Those who burst out laughing and ran after Francis remained in the brotherhood.

Of Larks and Sparrows

To be in love with Jesus was to be in love with all creatures as well, for Jesus had made all creatures holy. When Jesus stepped into the Jordan, all water became sacred. For Francis everything that Jesus touched was forever spiritualized. If Jesus died on a cross, then all wood and every tree inspired him with awe. If Jesus looked at the fields and birds and blessed them with His eyes, then every field and every bird was sister and brother to Francis because Jesus was his brother and Jesus was his friend and Lord, who shared everything He had with Francis. The sun was his brother, the moon was his sister and both belonged to him. In fact, everything Francis saw or heard or felt or smelled or breathed was his, because nothing was his. He had fiercely rooted out of his heart all possessiveness and greed; and as Jesus had promised, all these things were given back to him, pressed down and overflowing with love.

Because he possessed nothing, he was possessed by all the free creatures of God. All of creation loved him, every bird and animal, and Francis knew it and loved them in return.

Francis loved most tenderly the larks of Umbria. In comparison to them as they soared high in the blue skies of spring, he was the merest sparrow of a man. Sparrow! How fitting a name for himself. A poor ragged little sparrow. That was Francis. Feathers ruffled and frayed at the ends, brown and plain, perching on the balconies of Assisi, chirping his love songs to the poor and meek, the outcasts and beggars who do not need a lark to make them happy. Even he, poor sparrow of faded brown, could cheer the meek who seldom raised their eyes high enough to see a lark magnificent in its soaring and swooping in the clear skies of freedom.

But Francis loved the larks and wanted by his singing to make larks of all people, to lift them up and free their spirits so they could fly with him and all the larks above. In the blue freedom of God's love, even a sparrow became a lark and fantasy and joy made everyone's dream come true. Yet it was more than fantasy. It was the promises of Jesus fulfilled here and now for those who would dare to believe.

To those who left all things, Jesus had promised eternal life and a hundredfold besides—*now!* Being a lark was a part of the hundredfold; and on a spring morning, lifting his eyes from the red poppies and yellow buttercups of the Umbrian valley to Mount Subasio in the east, Francis wondered if being a lark might not be the whole of it. What greater beauty and grace could there be? For surely a lark was the resurrected Christ on wings of celebration.

A Trinity of Towns

Poggio Bustone, Fonte Colombo, Greccio. Towns that hang like humanity itself to the sheer cliffs of God's love and mercy. At each of these mountain villages above the plain of Rieti Francis had felt the living presence of Jesus. They formed a high triangle of mystical experience that made possible his life of activity below. All his life he had known the tension between the vertical ascent to God and the horizontal journey of love reaching out to all on earth. He knew that without prayer true love was impossible, and he learned from living that without love prayer became self-centered and barren.

In the early years he had wanted to live alone with the Dream, high above the city, and his spirit groaned to know if this was in fact to be his calling in life. The decision to turn his back to the world and his face to God was too terrifying a move to make all by himself. So he sent Brother Masseo to seek the advice of the Lady Clare and her sisters and of Brother Sylvester, the man who talked with God. They both sent back to him what his heart had already told him: that God had not chosen him for the Dream alone, but to repair the Church which was falling into ruin. The Journey was essential to the Dream.

He received Brother Masseo's words kneeling on the ground; and although he thought such words would buckle his knees and keep him from rising, he felt instead the surge of the Spirit within him and he leapt to his feet with courage and joy. That very moment he set out, his arm around Masseo, to breathe forth the Spirit of God. He chose the region of Rieti in which to preach the Word of God, and high above that valley the three mountain retreats of Poggio Bustone, Fonte Colombo, and Greccio perched as on three vertical pillars reaching to Heaven, keeping the Dream in sight.

Perfect Joy

An Interlude From the 'Fioretti'

One day as Francis and Brother Leo trudged through the snow and mud on their way from Perugia to the little church of St. Mary of the Angels, a strange thing happened. But it wasn't that strange, really, because this sort of thing was happening more and more often. Francis started to play word games with Leo.

"Brother Leo, we have just had one of our most successful preaching trips, and I'm sure you are as happy as I am that God has worked so grandly through two poor men like us. But you know, Brother Leo, this is not the greatest joy in Christ."

"Oh, Father Francis, don't lead me on forever this time.

What *is* the greatest joy in Christ?"

Francis smiled to himself that Leo was beginning to tire of the little question-and-answer periods he usually conducted whenever they were on the road together. So in deference to Leo, even though he liked the other way better because it helped him to clarify his own ideas, Francis relented and got to the point immediately.

"Well, Brother Leo, when we finally plod up to the door of the Portiuncula and knock, if the Brother there does not recognize us and calls us bums and grows impatient because bums should always appear immediately after dinner or supper and should have wine on their breaths, if he then closes the door in our faces and we remain patient, then that is the beginning of joy. And if the brother beats us besides, and we love him for it, then that is perfect joy."

"But, Father Francis, he *will* recognize us and besides that is kind of a dumb example when you come right down to it. I would probably knock the brother's block off for closing the door in *your* face."

Francis was elated.

"Oh, Brother Leo, thank you for saying just the right thing, so I can get to the real point."

Leo was learning to lead Francis on more quickly than in the past. He hadn't believed a word of his response to Francis, but it made Francis so happy when he could share some new insight with Leo.

"Brother Leo, only the Spirit of Jesus would enable you to be patient. That kind of experience is our continual initiation. We have to be testing our spirits constantly. Are we still carnal or is the Spirit of God stronger in us than our own selfishness?"

"The conquest of ourselves can be perfected only in the spirit. If because of our selfishness the Spirit has left us, we once again give in to our violent natures and return evil for evil. Oh, Brother Leo, pray for me that the Spirit will never abandon me to my old self."

Brother Leo, for all Francis' simplicity, could not help weeping for this wholly sincere and intense man with a child's heart.

"Oh, Father Francis, never will the Spirit leave a man like you. Would that God would give me your faith and love. You,

Father Francis, sinful as you are, should pray for *me*."

Leo always said that Francis was sinful because Francis felt better if people saw him as he saw himself. At first Leo found this pose difficult, but as time went on, he began to see that what for most would be an unhealthy self-hatred, for Francis was simple acceptance of facts as he saw them, and his exuberance over the Spirit's filling his life made his own sinfulness of no importance whatsoever, so long as Leo did not forget to mention it. That's the way Francis was; he never became depressed over his sins but rejoiced always in Jesus and His Spirit within him. And Leo loved him for it.

An Old Story of Courtly Love

Sometimes Francis got things all mixed up in his mind: Lady Poverty and the Lady Clare, his marriage to one, his reverence for the other. But then maybe they were the same after all. Lady Clare would sometimes merge in his own mind with his first dream of Lady Poverty and their betrothal. Not that he ever confused the two and believed that he was wed to the Lady Clare. He had himself given her in marriage to Christ. But what Lady Clare stood for and inspired in him was so closely akin to his love for Poverty that she was an integral part of the Dream.

He seldom looked at the Lady Clare, not because he was prudish or anything like that. He hated that kind of fear, and besides, Brother Dominic was spending himself for the Church fighting just such an error among a group of people called the Albigensians.

But he felt so humbled and strangely reverent around Lady Clare because she was the bride of Jesus. How precious and special that made her.

One day, however, Lady Clare herself sent a message to the brothers that she wanted to see Francis alone, and would he come to San Damiano sometime soon? Well, naturally, Francis was all upset that he should have to go alone to speak to Clare. So he

49

asked Brother Leo to go with him.

Leo, of course, thought that this Bride-of-Christ thing was all right, but you didn't have to be downright silly about it. He told Francis that if Lady Clare had wanted to see Leo, she would have asked to see Leo. And if Francis was afraid of Clare, he should grow up, because Lady Clare was about as holy and prudent as anyone could possibly be. Besides, she was pretty, and it would do Francis good to talk to someone pretty for a change. Well, Francis really thought Leo must be losing his mind, which is the way he felt about Leo most of the time anyway.

"Brother Leo, it is not at all seemly for a little brother to be seen conversing with so noble a lady as Sister Clare."

"So who's going to see you? And even if the whole world did, who cares?"

"*I* do, Brother Leo. If we are little and humble as we profess to be, then we have no place in the presence of a great personage like the Lady Poverty—I mean the Lady Clare."

Well, Brother Leo told Francis years later that at that moment Francis' thinking had finally begun to click for him. So that was why Francis got so upset every time he had to go to San Damiano to speak to the nuns. It was because they were all tied up with his own mystical marriage to Lady Poverty. Lady Clare especially, as Christ's Bride, stood for something quite central in Francis' original Dream.

Clare was the Lady of the Castle to whom he dedicated his great deeds for Christ and who made his own marriage to Lady Poverty a part of the whole tradition of courtly love. According to that tradition, a lover, even though he was married to someone else, would be expected to be devoted to the Lady of the Castle. Only in this case the Lord of the Castle was Christ Himself. That meant that his meetings with Lady Clare were to be ever totally pure and modest, completely free of any kind of possession of her, even with his eyes. Francis had sublimated courtly love and transformed it, as he had all of Creation. Leo was again humbled and turned to Francis.

"Surely, Father, you are right. We must go together so that I can assure the absolute propriety of your conversation and even speak for you if necessary since I am older and more learned than such a poor knight as you."

Francis wept aloud that Leo so thoroughly understood, and

the two rode off on imaginary steeds to the great hall of Damiano castle.

The Wolf of Gubbio

Francis loved the woods. He wasn't sentimental about them, though. In fact, what Francis loved most about the out-of-doors was that everything was there—good and evil, danger and refuge, violence and peace. So he wasn't at all minimizing the danger to the citizens of Gubbio. After all, a wolf was a wolf, and he was not so naive as to confuse a wolf with a dog.

As soon as he had heard the news of the wolf of Gubbio, Francis felt sympathy for the wolf. There was something of the wolf in all of nature, that ravenous hunger, that restless pursuit, that baring of the fangs, so symbolic of what was wild and violent in all of us. But he saw in the wolf not so much the stalker as the stalked. Everyone feared wolves and disliked them, and he saw in the eyes of wolves a fear, a hunted look, an anger and hostility that wanted to devour everything in sight in order to avenge their own hurt and alienation. Wolves, after all, were like people. If you feared them and ostracized them and excluded them, they eventually turned into what you were afraid they were anyway.

The Gubbio affair, however, was even more interesting to Francis, because this was not a pack of wolves banded together for security and strength. This was one lone wolf. One deserter from the pack, striking back all by himself. Solitary, panicked into rage and violence. Francis thought of Cain fleeing east of Eden, branded, an outsider, cut off from society.

He knew that he had to go up to Gubbio, to communicate in some way with this outrageously courageous wolf. If only the wolf would recognize Francis' admiration and let Francis prove his acceptance of him as one of the mad, angry creatures of God. Surely this wolf would prefer adventure and usefulness and belonging to the loneliness of the dark woods and streets, the light of the town's respect to the shadows of its fear.

So Francis once again set out from Assisi on the high road to Gubbio.

He no sooner entered the city than he heard the buzzing of rumor about the wolf. That in itself would be enough to anger most creatures. He was glad the wolf couldn't understand human speech, because he remembered how desolate and depressed he had felt at the beginning when he changed his way of life and his fellow Assisians had mocked him and jeered at his rough tunic, his beard, his unkempt appearance. He felt more a brother to the wolf than to these terrified citizens of Gubbio.

Before the gossip created more fear and anger, he would have to do something dramatic. So Francis walked bravely to the piazza and started to preach to the people about the command of Jesus to love all creatures of God. Then, in the middle of his sermon, he hinted that as he entered the city, he had heard rumors of a wild wolf that was known to steal into the town from time to time and kill little children. Everyone began shouting at once, assuring him that, "*Si, Si,*" this was true.

Then in a moment of bravado that scared Francis after he had said it, he asked them if anyone knew where the wolf's lair was, that he would like to see this wolf and prove to the wolf and to all of them that love had nothing to do with fear.

The townsfolk were dumbfounded, and some rough men began to laugh out loud. Francis was used to that sort of thing, so he just waited until they had all got the laugh out of their systems and a hush had fallen upon the square. Then a fat little woman stepped forward, and spitting at the feet of a huge ox of a man, said she would take Francis out of the town and show him the lair. No one laughed; the big man turned red with rage. Francis bowed to the little lady as to a countess, and she demurely curtsied back as she took Francis by the hand. The two walked right through the crowd and up the street toward the gates on top of the hill that led to the Shrine of St. Ubaldo.

By this time the crowd had regained their composure, and the men especially were furious that they had seemed like cowards in front of their wives and daughters, who were already beginning to fall in line behind Francis and the woman. So they, too, started for the city gates.

In true Italian fashion, the anger wore off quickly and everyone seemed to be caught up in the excitement of the procession as though they were going on some grand pilgrimage. Francis was elated, though still a bit shaken by his hasty challenge to meet the wolf. As always, when he was a little nervous, he began to sing, and soon the whole crowd was belting out an old marching song. They soon came to a turn in the road and the woman pointed to an overhanging rock that lay about 500 yards ahead. "Under that," she said proudly and inched closer to Francis. The woman had become a folk heroine in her own mind, and she seemed determined not to relinquish her position next to Francis. Francis thought the woman a real character, the kind of solid matron who would have fought off the whole crowd to protect him and never expect a word of thanks. He was convinced of this and he wanted her to share any glory there might be from this foolhardy escapade, so he asked her to go with him to the cave.

The woman accepted without batting an eye, picked up her skirts, and thumbed her nose at the man who had laughed in the marketplace. The two set out arm in arm for the lair, and the crowd stood back, scratching their heads and shrugging their shoulders. The big man began to take bets and soon large-scale gambling was opening up right there in the middle of the field.

Meanwhile Francis and the woman were drawing close to the rock. Suddenly, without warning, they heard behind them a low growl and a pounding of the ground. Spinning around, Francis saw the wolf charging wildly toward them. Francis made the sign of the cross, first over the petrified woman and then over the wolf. He took a deep breath and started walking slowly toward him. The wolf slowed his pace and then came to an abrupt stop.

Francis walked on. The wolf was frothing at the mouth and growling menacingly. The crowd stood motionless and silent. Francis stopped a few yards from the wolf and stared at him as kindly as he could under the circumstances.

Anger flashed in the wolf's eyes and he was working his jaws, slobbering onto the ground. Francis dared not move now that he was face-to-face with the wolf. He stood still and tried to look calm. Then he said simply and in a low, quiet voice, "Brother Wolf." The wolf quieted down in an apparent response to Francis' words. The wolf stared at him and beyond him to the woman who was frozen to the same spot, her mouth open, her hands clasped before her in an attitude of prayer or defense. Francis spoke again. "Brother Wolf, in the name of Jesus, our brother, I have come for you. We need you in the city. These people here have come with me to ask you, great ferocious one, to be the guardian and protector of Gubbio. In return we offer you respect and shelter for as long as you live. In pledge of this I offer you my hand."

He stretched out his hand. The wolf seemed calm, but he remained immobile, scanning the crowd with his large, bloodshot eyes. Then slowly he walked to Francis and lifted his paw into his warm, steady hand. The two remained in that position for a long time and what they said to one another Francis never told to any living soul.

Finally, Francis leaned over and put his arms about the wolf's neck. Then he and his new brother walked meekly up to the brave peasant woman and the three of them led the stunned, silent crowd back to Gubbio.

Signatures in the Air

Little lizards dart across the walls of Assisi, zig-zagging quick patterns of their movements on tawny stone. Their green bodies against the pink and red made the whole wall interesting and alive.

Francis saw himself in these little creatures that shoot back and forth, in and out of the tiny crevices. They loved the geography of their little world and they went about the business of their lives unselfconsciously, totally preoccupied with the humble stone.

It was their movement that fascinated him. Their motion was a pattern scribbled in the air which disappeared as soon as it was made. There was no permanence in these tiny signatures, no monument to themselves left behind. That is what he wanted to be: a tiny signature in the air that thrilled someone who saw it, but was as anonymous as a lizard's zig-zagged darting on a pink Assisi wall. His movement would be his poem.

Knight of the Round Table

April in Assisi. It always seemed to be raining then. Everyone stayed indoors about the fireplace, cozy and comfortable, and told stories and ate and drank warming wine. Everyone except the very poor and the Lesser Brothers. For them, on the plain at St. Mary of the Angels, there was only dampness and rain water washing down the walls and filling the huts with mud puddles. Then it was that Francis felt closest to his brothers. He wanted them to taste this delicious savor of poverty, and he felt somehow like Moses, leading the Israelites out of the comfortableness of Egypt into the desert.

In the beginning the brothers welcomed rainy days, and cold, damp nights, but as the number of brothers grew, so did the complaining. Francis began to feel guilty, not because the brothers suffered, but because some were insulting Lady Poverty to her face. He felt guilty before her that some of his own brothers would so little understand the Dream. The Dream, after all, had never been presented to them as easy or comfortable. On the contrary, Francis insisted that the Rule of the Lesser Brothers was to live the rigor of the Gospel of Jesus Christ, who had nowhere to lay His head.

Francis understood the pain of the brothers, but it was unfathomable to him that they should utter that pain so loudly. And discouraging and critical words always grew in the community like a cancer affecting even the strongest brothers. That is why Francis loved Brother Giles so much. He always had words of encouragement and wisdom that sowed peace and love among the brothers. Francis called Giles, "The Knight of the Round Table," for he was totally devoted to the Lady Poverty; he was chaste, and he was ever cheerful as befitted a Knight of Christ.

Cheerfulness! How totally selfless one must be to remain cheerful. There was so much hardship and so many distasteful things attached to the knighthood of Poverty, that the biggest temptation was to bitterness and a disgruntled heart. The true brother of the Dream welcomed, most of all, humiliation and misunderstanding and rejoiced in it. The first brothers understood that and went out of their way to make themselves look foolish.

And it was Brother Giles who put that wisdom into words. Leo was collecting the sayings of Brother Giles, and he told Francis that someday people would read them and weep that so much wisdom should be found in so lowly a knight as Brother Giles of the Lesser Brothers of Assisi. And Francis was happy.

These are the sayings of Brother Giles that Francis kept close to his heart:

Blessed are you who love and don't expect to be loved in return.

Blessed are you who fear and don't want to be feared.

Blessed are you who serve and don't expect to be served in return.

Blessed are you who treat others well and don't expect like treatment in return.

Because these are profound truths the foolish do not rise to them.

If you possess these three qualities, you cannot be evil: first, if, for God's sake, you bear in peace all tribulation that comes your way; second, if you humble yourself in everything you do and receive; third, if you love faithfully those things that cannot be seen with fleshly eyes.

The trouble with many people is that they hate what they should love and love what they should hate.

Holy contrition, holy humility, holy charity, holy devotion, and holy joy make you holy and good.

How well Brother Giles understood the Dream. He was truly one of the Knights of the Round Table.

A Gallery of Portraits

In his mind Francis kept little pictures of the first brothers. They were frescoes he would like to have painted on the walls of the Portiuncula, the Little Portion, as he affectionately called his tiny church of St. Mary of the Angels. The colors would all be bright and cheerful and they would bring to life the poverty of Bernard of Quintavalle, the purity and simplicity of Leo, the chastity of Angelo, the intelligence and eloquence of Masseo, the mystical mind of Giles, the prayerful spirit of Rufino, the patience of Juniper, the strength of soul and body of John de Laudibus, the loving nature of Roger of Todi, the pilgrim soul of Lucidus. What a pantheon of perfection that would be. It would be a pageant in plaster of the Journey and the Dream. In these men everything Francis loved and believed in took flesh. And if anyone would want to come to the brothers and join their Order, then he must first look at these frescoes in detail to know what is expected of the ideal Lesser Brother.

Francis would paint them so softly that no one would draw back in fear and say he could not live that heroically. No, he would say rather, "Would that God might grant me the calling to join hands with these happy, carefree men of God. For they speak truly to my heart of what I have always longed to become." Oh, how great the hand of the artist that could make this merry company of brothers live forever, and how Francis wished he could be that blessed man and give that lovely gift to these his truest sharers in the Dream.

But he could not paint, nor could he sculpt except with words. So to Brother Leo he dictated a letter addressed to all the brothers in which he described the ideal Lesser Brother, and in his letter the little frescoes came to life, and he mentioned all 10 brothers by name. He wanted all the brothers to know that the Dream could be lived and was in fact being lived right then in these imperfect but faithful brothers.

He saw the embarrassment of Leo's face the moment that he began to copy down Francis' words. But Francis would tolerate no opposition nor any scruple on any brother's part in this sacred matter touching the practicality of the Dream. He had heard too often the argument that no one could really live the

Rule of Life that Jesus Himself had whispered in his ear. That real men were living it, he hoped would be enough to make people pause and think. And if they still mocked the Dream, then they had turned their hearts away from the witness of 10 holy lives, and they were incapable of dreaming and longing and growing into the Ideal.

Dream of Flight

Winging. Running. Fighting the sluggishness of his own weight upon the earth. Smiling as he scaled the rough side of mountains. Was this madness, this perpetual dream of flying? The very act of lifting his arms seemed to free him of the pull of the earth below him.

He loved the earth, but his motion was always up and away from it toward some intangible tug at his heart from above. He felt at times like a puppet caught in the middle of a tug-of-war between invisible forces he did not understand. And they were both pulling from inside his own heart. O the secret scars of those opposing ropes through his heart! O the release of the upward sweep of the arms!

The open palms of his hands, especially, released him from the knotted tangle within. The open palms. The attitude of Christ on the cross, vulnerable, open, pouring Himself out for us. The cross! God's final pull of victory over the opposing forces in the heart.

He clutched his small wooden cross to his heart and felt he was flying again.

Memories of a Shopkeeper's Son

Francis had loved working in his father's shop. The cloth he sold was beautiful and of fine quality, and he felt proud of all the merchandise in the store. Besides, it was so much fun joking with the housewives and young girls and making them blush by describing with grand exaggeration what this piece of purple taffeta would do for their appearance. At times he would play the clown and drape an expensive piece of Venetian damask over his shoulder and strut around the store mimicking one of the local nobles to the delight of some young lady who would giggle and try to hide her affection for Francis.

Francis knew, of course, that he was one of the major reasons for his father's booming business. Every young girl in town came to the shop as much to see him as to buy cloth. And Francis had loved it. He treated every one as if she were the sole object of his attention, and the girls left the store elated and weighted down with cloth to the "Thank you, my lovely" of Pietro, who stood in the door twirling his moustache and beaming from ear to ear.

However, the more cloth that piled up in the chests of Assisi's nobles, the more frustrated the girls became. No one of them could claim Francis as her own or elicit from Francis even the slightest hint of an advance. But he was so gallant that they found him irresistible and continued to come and try their luck with this young charmer and flatterer with the flashing black eyes and contagious good humor.

One day when Francis was busily preoccupied with a fat and wealthy matron, a beggar sidled up to him and butted rudely into the conversation. Francis, offended both by the rudeness and by the dirty appearance of the man, curtly dismissed him and turned back to the woman. The beggar, surprised by this kind of treatment from the reputedly generous Francis, grumbled and cursed and left the shop in a huff, spitting on the cobblestones in front of the store.

Francis, in the meantime, was trying to convince the pompous woman that this new French cloth would certainly make her look 10 pounds slimmer. But his attention was not really on the woman. Already he regretted his peremptory dismissal of the miserable beggar. The woman asked him if there was anything wrong; he seemed distracted and ill. Francis paused.

"Well, yes. As a matter of fact there is something wrong. Excuse me, signora."

And with that he left the stunned woman standing there with a bolt of French silk and Pietro running from the back room to rescue the embarrassing situation.

Years later Francis told Brother Leo this incident and added, "Brother Leo, I felt so small that day. If the beggar had asked for alms in the name of some count, I would have asked the woman to excuse me for a minute and I would have given the man a handsome sum. But, instead, I resented this uncouth behavior when I was talking to an important lady. But when he left, all I could hear drumming in my ears was the remark with which the beggar prefaced his request, 'For the love of God.' That was the first time, Brother Leo, that I realized I had been generous in order to win human praise and so that I would ingratiate myself with people. But the love of God I was willing to postpone until *after* an important business deal. The revelation was like an epiphany, a shining, glorious revelation from God. It hit me immediately and deeply and put my mind in a spin until I couldn't stand it any longer and ran from the shop after the still disgruntled beggar. How stunned he was when I caught up with him and literally poured the gold coins into his shaking palms. It was the first time that I really felt free and close to God."

And Brother Leo said, yes, he understood. The same feeling had come over *him* the first time he had heard Francis preach about the poor Christ. "I ran out of the church, Francis, and gave all the coins I had with me to a beggar whose corner I had avoided for years because the man was such an aggressive and repulsive pest. And Jesus clutched my heart, and I knew that I must somehow come to you and live with you, the man through whom the Lord had finally found me."

That mutual revelation was the beginning of a friendship that was to last into eternity, and now, as Francis lay dying, he was comforted by the thought that Leo was there with him. And Leo would suffer with him, so that all the pain was halved by Leo's love. He turned his head and smiled at tough and practical Brother Leo, who was now weeping unabashedly in front of the younger brothers. Francis was pleased and a little tickled that Leo, who was always telling Francis to stop his eternal weeping, was now weeping himself. And even Leo's tears seemed strong and manly.

Of Leo and Francis

Francis and Leo stood on the coast of Ancona, looking out to sea. The gulls screamed above the crashing of surf on the rocks, and Francis knew he had heard those screams before, but he did not remember when or where. It must have been a long, long time ago, perhaps when he was a boy on one of the trips with his father. His father! What had become of him, and of his mother, so quiet and lovely, standing always in his memory at the threshold of his room, looking in, smiling and comforting his moods with her presence?

Brother Leo noticed the far-away look in Francis' eyes and said nothing. He only looked at the sea and hoped Francis would again share his thoughts with him.

"Brother Leo," Francis said haltingly, "I left my father for Our Father in Heaven, and I've never mentioned his name since. But here, looking at the ocean and hearing the cry of the gulls, I weep for him and I pray for him and for Lady Pica, my mother. Brother Leo, I still love them so much. Those saints are cold who say we can forget all our loves in the love of God. I cannot. All my loves are caught up in my Lord and made perfect in Him. I neither forget my loves nor cease to love once I've given my heart. Brother Leo, can you understand that?"

Brother Leo only nodded and reached down and picked up a stone and hurled it into the sea. And Francis understood that Brother Leo, too, could never fully distract himself from all that had been. He was Leo and Francis was Francis and here on the coast of Italy, looking South, a further bond had grown between them. Francis reached down and took a smooth white stone and flung it into the sea, and they walked together down to the Crusaders' boats where he would leave Brother Leo behind and set sail for the Holy Land.

Francis Before the Sultan

The upward lift of the sea breeze buoyed Francis' spirit, and he felt expanded, almost inflated with the anticipation of seeing his brothers again, despite the rumors that had reached him of deviations from his strict Rule of Poverty. There he was again, thinking of *his* Rule. He must remember that the Order was not his personal property or he would end up giving up everything material in order to possess *men*. How terrible that would be, yet how real a temptation! And besides, the rumors were probably far worse than the real situation. Anyway, he was still a good distance from the Italian Coast, and he was feeling like St. Paul returning from a great missionary journey to straighten out some misunderstanding that had developed during his absence.

As the boat bounced uncertainly on the choppy little waves, Francis caught the staccato rhythm, and he let himself relax in the forward bumping of the little boat. The beating of the waves reminded him of the thumping of his heart at the camp of the Sultan. Now, his desire to meet the Sultan face-to-face seemed in retrospect rather foolish, but foolishness, after all, was the point of the whole trip. He had wanted as much to impress his brothers with Gospel foolishness as he had wanted to tell the Sultan about Jesus and about the peaceful inner cavern he had found.

He was terrified when he had finally been ushered into the Sultan's presence, and he wondered about all that equanimity stuff the saints were supposed to have had whenever a crisis arose. But he marched steadily forward, never dropping his eyes and staring openly into the Sultan's iron eyes. Francis was shaken by the scowl on the Sultan's face. He reminded Francis a little of his own father, that fierce concentration in his eyes, the drooping jowls, and the long oval ears.

As Francis drew nearer, the Sultan's expression changed to one of mild amusement. Francis couldn't help returning the expression. This seemed to please the Sultan because when Francis stopped in front of him, the two were grinning at each other. The sycophants around the Sultan were also grinning broadly until the Sultan turned and frowned; then they frowned back like little mirrors.

"Well, little man, I see you have courage. I watched your nervous walk and steady eyes, and I said to myself, him I would like at my court. He would tell me the truth, and not what I usually hear."

He emphasized the last few words, his eyes roaming coldly over his own courtiers. Francis said nothing.

"I see you also have manners. I like that."

There was a long pause, embarrassing only to the courtiers who shifted from foot to foot and coughed tensely.

"Well, holy man, what do you want of me?"

"Only to bring you peace, great one."

The Sultan smiled. "But I like war, little Italian. For Allah I am conquering the world. It is why I was born and why I am Allah's instrument."

"But, great Prince, I am not talking about peace as the opposite of war. I speak of peace in your heart, a deep satisfaction and joy that flows from within like a rich wine."

"And what, to a warrior, can bring more inner peace than victory on the battlefield?"

"Prayer, O child of Allah."

"Prayer? And do I not pray every day to Allah?"

"More, I am sure, great leader, than many Christians pray.

"But I want to share with you a prayer I learned by fighting the great battle with my self, by conquering one by one the demons in my own heart. Your prayer is good, I am sure, but I want to teach you a new prayer."

"Then pray it for me now, here in front of these dullards who infest my tent."

Francis knelt down and lifted up his eyes, beyond the dais to a small opening in the tent that let the light in.

Lord, make me an instrument of your peace.
Where there is hatred let me sow love.
Where there is injury, pardon;
Where there is doubt, faith;
Where there is despair, hope;
Where there is darkness, light;
And where there is sadness, joy.

O Divine Master

Let me not so much seek to be consoled
As to console;
To be understood as to understand;
To be loved as to love.

For it is in giving that we receive,
It is in pardoning that we are pardoned,
And it is in dying that we are born to eternal life.

The Sultan said nothing. He seemed moved by what Francis had poured from his heart. Yes, it was like a good rich wine.

In a soft voice, so that only Francis could hear, he said. "Oh, little beggar and man of dreams. I wish in my heart that there were more gentle men like you to balance the hatred in the world. Unfortunately, the world understands only two things: power and violence. Some day, your prayer says to me, the world will be turned upside down by little folk who fast and pray and who die rather than take up the sword. Till then, God's will is performed through violent men like me."

"Will you, Lord Sultan, pray for that day?"

"I will do more, honest man, I will let you walk out of this camp alive, so that *you* can pray for that day. I pray that after I am gone from this earth (but not before) Allah will change his mind and use meek instruments like you and that this great army of peace-loving beggars will outnumber the forces of hatred and violence. Go to your dreams, brave little man."

Then aloud the Sultan said, "Take this fool from our camp and give him safe passage to his own kind. I will not lower myself by harming beggars and vermin and threadbare Christians. You can see from the man's appearance how badly we have beaten down the Christians. Go."

He winked at Francis, and Francis smiled back, and in the strictest adherence to chivalrous conduct, backed out of the room.

Just then the little boat came about and broke the rhythm of Francis' thoughts. His eyes focused in on the horizon again, and he saw the blessed land of Italy rising up before him. He was indeed home again even if, as a pilgrim and a stranger, he was not supposed to be at home anywhere. How deep the feelings lie, and no amount of preaching can change what is real and good, he thought.

Of Citizens and Beggars

The quiet of the Umbrian Valley. The security of the narrow, fortified streets of Assisi. He hoped that his life, in disturbing the order of things, had not destroyed the silence and peace of Umbria. But he knew that for a while the brothers had turned Assisi and the whole Umbrian Valley upside down. And he had intended that they should do just that, for a time.

Francis always loved the simple Umbrian peasant. But a new kind of society had arisen in the city and a new kind of citizen was emerging. These citizens of the city were killing the lover in their own hearts because they were turning everything and everyone into objects to be used for their own personal advancement. Money especially was becoming the means of climbing the ladder of importance and prestige in society.

From the plain of St. Mary of the Angels, Assisi itself had for a while seemed like a huge castle with citizens clawing at one another and throwing each other to the ground as they strove to reach the uppermost battlements and control the whole castle and the valley below it. And Francis reflected that he, too, had almost become a part of that scramble to the top. He had as a young man always been treated like a nobleman because his father was extremely wealthy. He remembered the first time he went to war for the citizens of Assisi in the battle against Perugia. He was captured at the skirmish of Ponte San Giovanni and spent a year in a Perugian prison, not with the rest of the soldiers, but with the noblemen.

The society of Assisi was divided into the *majores* and the *minores*, and Francis had moved from the "greater ones" to the "lesser ones" when he finally met Jesus. He called his brotherhood the *Fratres Minores*, the Lesser Brothers, and he wanted them always to be associated with the poor, the lesser people in society. That desire was a constant source of amazement to people, for all wanted to "better" their condition and become more wealthy and comfortable as they built solidly for the future. Money was the foundation of their faith, securing their castles against the storms of circumstances and fate. Francis and the brothers had battered against these frail foundations, and in the course of years, many in Umbria had come to see that the brothers were right.

At first the people scoffed at them and complained bitterly of these lazy bums who lived off the responsible, respectable citizenry. Sure, these brothers "gave up" everything all right. But the next day they were at your door begging for a share of what you worked so hard to provide for your family. They must think that Assisi is a tiered layer cake baked into the side of Mount Subasio that they can cut into anytime they like.

But later the example of the brothers won out, and the citizens considered them essential witnesses in their midst. To Francis, the most gratifying example of their change of heart came when he returned from the Holy Land and called the first major gathering of the brothers. Five thousand of them met at St. Mary of the Angels. For eight days, they lived in the open air or in little huts of woven boughs, and such a huge crowd was anything but a model spectacle of cleanliness and order. But despite the unkempt appearance of this motley crew of beggars, the citizens of Assisi now knew that they were real leaven. The brothers had been faithful to Lady Poverty and in return the townsfolk showered them with food and considered it a privilege to do so. How great the power of the Gospel Life when lived sincerely and unconditionally!

He remembered telling Leo and Angelo and Masseo, "You can be sure, brothers, that the more we are ashamed of Lady Poverty, the more people will hate us; but if we embrace her as closely as we can, people will love us for it." And they had: Down all the roads the brothers had carried the standard of their Lady Poverty. And peace and security remained with those who saluted the tattered flag of the Brothers Poor of Assisi.

Of Monastery Builders

Once in the morning when the sun was striking the cream cliffs of Greccio, he had seen in the bright flash of light the whole of his cave illuminated and he felt warm. That fire of sun is what he wished for his brothers. Lately, in the dark and damp of his caves, he thought he sensed what some of his brothers would feel in the brotherhood. They would be cold and damp and there would be no sun to warm the dark corners of their lives. The brotherhood, he feared, would grow too big for them to cope with. And these would be men of the Journey, made sad by a brotherhood that did not move.

Already the inroads of the monastery-builders were clearing the tangled undergrowth to the brothers' huts. When he was away in Egypt, some of the brothers started to build a monastery right next to the holy church of the Portiuncula, the mother church of Lady Poverty. He remembered the tears in his eyes and the shamed look in the brothers' eyes when he returned unexpectedly from the Holy Land and climbed to the top of the half-finished building. He began wildly throwing the stones to the ground, seeing in every one a millstone dragging his brothers down into the abyss. He had to free them from these stones that would be the end of the Journey and the beginning of pain for those who would ride the swift horses of God's Heralds.

And he wondered who would be there when he was gone to hurl to the ground the stones of complacency and mediocrity. He knew in that flash of sun at Greccio that there would be no one strong enough to keep so many brothers moving. And he cried aloud to Christ to save the Journey. But all he saw reflected on the walls was Assisi and Poggio Bustone and Fonte Colombo and Greccio as one huge shrine of stones. And he wept aloud for the brothers of the Journey and for the Lady Clare, for she would see the shrine grow before her very eyes.

And then in the final flash of the sun's morning rays, he saw on his cave the reflections of a great procession of moving figures, and they seemed in the shadows on the wall to wear a robe and cord. He prayed it was not an illusion.

Christmas at Greccio

Someone to love, someone to care for. It was that thought which gripped his heart at Greccio that Christmas he had decided to celebrate the Birth of Jesus in a new way. He had brought a real ox and ass to the altar so that they, too, could share in this rebirth of Christ in the bread and wine of the Christmas Eucharist.

At Christmas it was the infant Christ who was born again in human hearts, and it struck Francis that God came to earth as a baby so that we would have someone to care for. Christmas was the dearest of feasts because it meant that God was now one of us. Flesh of our flesh and bone of our bone, this child we could approach without fear. We could be silly and uninhibited as we sought to make Him laugh. We could be totally ourselves because a child accepts us just as we are and screams with delight at our little performances in his behalf.

Someone to care for, someone to try and please, someone to love. God, a helpless babe; God, a piece of Bread. How much trust God had in creatures! In the Eucharist and in the Nativity, we grow up, because God places Himself in our care. We come out of ourselves if we are aware, because we now have responsibilities for God. Not only the earth to till and creation to subdue, but now God to care for.

And so strong was Francis' desire to love, that at that Christmas Mass at Greccio the babe of Bethlehem appeared to him alive and smiling on the cold rock.

And he took the babe into his arms and held it to his heart, and the child was warm and soft. Francis' virginity was made fruitful in this child he held to his breast. He had no child but Jesus Himself. His Lord had reversed the roles for him and for all who need someone to love, someone to care for.

The peasants at that Mass had witnessed Francis' fatherhood, and the child became theirs as well. They had brought torches for their midnight journey from the village on the hill opposite the brothers' hermitage. But they did not need them for the journey home that night, so brightly did their own hearts burn that God had truly been enfleshed in the baby at the altar. Francis was so happy for them. These simple folk from Greccio were like children themselves, and God had once again been revealed to little ones.

Someone to love. That was Greccio, that was Christmas. He prayed for all the lonely people of the world that they would understand what God's enfleshment meant to them personally. God was like us now in everything but sin. And He let Himself be touched and handled by everyone who would come to Him. Someone to care for, someone to touch. That was Greccio, that was God become a man.

Francis left Greccio that year with a new heart, for the

brothers would keep alive the custom of celebrating Christmas in that fashion. And the people of Greccio would spread the word to the next village, and from there it would cover the whole of Italy and maybe the world. Someday, perhaps, all people could look into the altar creche at Christmas and know they had someone special to love, someone divine to care for. And they would begin anew to love.

Working With His Hands

The touch of the grain of wood, the feel of plants to the hand, the brush of wheat shocks against the leg. All these real and natural things Francis loved. Toward the end of his life he dictated his last will, his Testament, to Brother Leo and he wanted to put everything he had learned into those last encouraging words to his brothers.

"This line, Brother Leo, is most important to me. So write it tenderly, write it well: 'I worked with my hands and I want all my brothers to work with their hands.'"

Francis remembered the melancholy times when depression had settled down and moved in like an unwanted guest that you don't know how to get rid of. He would then roll up his sleeves and plunge himself into exhausting physical work. He saw himself carrying, one by one, the large stones that were to hold up the crumbling St. Mary of the Angels, the little church that he loved so much. As he placed one stone upon another, the order of stone on stone seemed to order the chaos within. And when the last rock was mortared into place, Francis felt secure. He had accomplished something; he had built order, he had won the battle against confusion and despair.

The memory of the weeks and months he had spent as a helping hand in the fields around Assisi still warmed these colder days of his last illness. He loved the feel of soil beneath him and the brush of grass and weeds across his open sandals. And he worked hard, never expecting any pay, but afterwards begging food from some other farm people. That way, begging and hard work were one. He did not feel justified in begging bread of anyone unless he had put in a hard day's work. But he always tried to beg from someone who would not know he had been working in the fields all day. The farmer, then, would be giving Francis food for the love of Jesus and not because Francis had "earned" it. He feared laziness and idleness. Yet some days he had worked hardest just trying to find work. And if at the end of day, he was still seeking employment, he would then go confidently for alms, knowing he had worked harder than when he had spent twelve hours in the fields.

The anxiety of wanting work, but finding none, always left him empty and feeling useless. And he would have to slow down and remind himself of Jesus' promise to provide for him even more than he had for the lilies of the field. Sometimes he would see lilies shriveled up or birds dead by the side of the road, and he would be afraid. His only comfort then was that the birds and lilies had not worried about their deaths beforehand. He should not either if he wanted to be free. Death would come when it would come, and he would cease upon some moment of ecstasy like a high-flying lark, shot in mid-air and crashing to the ground. His spirit would then leave the feathers behind and soar back in the blue cloudless skies of freedom, knowing he was now eternally immune to the arrows of any suffering or pain or death.

Francis had hoped that his moment of ecstasy would be while he was working in a field. But Brother Ass, as he always called his body, gave out too soon, and he had been unable to work for some time now.

Ironically, this non-activity was the hardest work he had ever done. For now nothing remained but love, kept alive by his faith and his hope. He had never been so utterly dependent on others. This was Lady Poverty's last courtship of him, and he realized for the first time that honeymoons do recur to those who persevere in love to the end. He now submitted finally and totally to his Lady, giving up for her even the pride of honest labor. And he was at peace in her arms.

Of Love

Where is Love? Can it be found somewhere along the way like some treasure that makes the Journey worthwhile? Or is love the Journey itself? Or is it the Dream that makes the Journey possible? These thoughts ran through Francis' mind one day as he listened to Brother Leo reading to him the Letter of John the Apostle: "God is love, and if you abide in love, you abide in God and God in you."

Yes, if you found God, you also found love. But that was only the beginning of the Quest, for who was ever sure of having found God or even sure of looking for God in the right places and by the right road? Francis' experience in the cave assured him that Jesus dwelled within him, that God was nowhere farther than his own heart. But there were other Presences of God he sought to find. He wanted to search for God in all the places where He dwelled and he knew that such a quest meant finding God everywhere along the way.

That is where love was, that is where God was—anywhere and everywhere. To find God in the poor crumbling houses of Poggio Bustone, to find God in the castle of a count, and in a cave on Mount Subasio, as well as in the Eucharist reserved in the tiny chapel of St. Mary of the Angels. Francis suddenly realized that somewhere along the way he had begun finding God everywhere because God was with him all the time. He brought love with him on the road and that is why he found love all along the way.

It was all so simple when he thought about it now. Love comes to those who have Love already. You find what you bring with you in your heart. God has first loved us and that gift is ours before we ever set out to find it. That secret was there already in the prayer he taught the Sultan, but he had not understood it quite the way he did the day he heard the Letter of John from Leo's lips.

It was often that way with his prayers. He would not even understand his own words, for they would well up and spill over into words that came from the deep center within him that held secrets he did not know that he knew. It was only later when he had prayed the words and thought about their meaning that they would one day come clear, and he would understand them as he never did before. Perhaps that insight, that secret brought to light, is why he continued to pray even when the words no longer meant anything to him. He was waiting for the flash of light, that spark of the Spirit, which would illumine once again the darkness of his mind and warm the heart within him that was cold.

Those insights, like the one he had while Leo read John's Letter, carried him for years upon the road, and every now and then he would understand the mystery of Love in still another way, and he would kneel upon the road wherever he was and thank the Holy Spirit for this gift of understanding.

Barefoot in the Dirt

One of the hardest trials of poverty, that sometimes made Francis forget how glorious was the service of his Lady Poverty, was the inconvenience of the poor life. To be poor was to be subject to countless little annoyances that the lords, or even the rich merchants like his father, could buy their way out of.

To be poor was to take the road on foot while the rich rode. To be poor was to wait long hours in the shops while the rich went before you. To be poor was to beg and eat what was placed before you, and that monotonously the same gruel, while the rich ate at tables ever varying their fare. To be poor was to mingle with those who were petty, narrow-minded and whose conversation was dull and uninspired, while the rich chose companions with care and welcomed the educated, the artist, the entertainer. To be poor was to live among those who had given up hope and whose lives were lived from moment to moment with no star to lead them on, while the rich still had ambition and the will to accomplish something in life.

The earthiness of it all, the gritty, day-to-day reality of poverty was what would kill the Dream for many. Even some of his brothers were already compromising their commitment to Lady Poverty. Their idealism could not withstand the reality below the Dream. And because they could not embrace the grime and inconvenience, they lost the arms of Lady Poverty as well. For union with her was achieved only in the sacred penetration of dirt when you wanted to be clean, of a cold stone slab when you wanted a warm bed, of sleeping alone when you wanted someone beside you, of the will of others when your own was wiser and more efficient, of routine when you longed for variety.

But if you had faith enough to love a lady so patently ugly and repulsive, in the consummation, in the emptying of yourself in her, she was transformed into the most enchanting Lady of your dreams. That was her secret, and that was the precious, hidden message you took with you on the Journey. Along the way you always found someone whose heart was pure enough to share the secret with. And the company of your lady's lovers grew quietly among those who Dreamed while walking barefoot in the dirt.

An Apologia for Penance

What brings one to penance and mortification? Is there any sense or reason behind renunciation and austerity? Why would anyone embrace the pain of separation as a way of life? Francis knew that people had these questions on their minds when they met the brothers. And especially did people wonder when men like Bernard of Quintavalle, the merchant, and Peter Catani, the lawyer, left their professions and belongings behind and attached themselves to Francis.

To explain it was perhaps impossible, but it had something to do with restoring harmony within themselves and between themselves and their Creator. It was like a search for the Garden of Eden before the Fall. That Garden was the end of the Journey, and they of course knew it was not an attainable goal. Or was it? That was the question. In each of them there was the Dream of discovering within themselves a secret source of energy, a Presence that would transform their lives and restore the harmony of the Garden of Paradise.

They would still be human, subject to temptation and sickness, sin and death, but in listening to the One who stood at the door within and knocked, they would open the doors of their own hearts and experience the Divine Presence that stood at the center of their real selves. And there they would walk again with

God in the cool of the evening. They would be united with God on a new level of consciousness and understanding.

So the pain of detachment was only a means of union. It was a way of stilling, of quieting everything that would prevent them from hearing that hushed knock of God within. That is why Francis had left his father. Pietro's world, his values and what he lived for, clamored so loud in Francis' ears, he could not hear the Voice in the heart of his real self. That is why he was willing and able to bear the insults and hooting of the citizens of Assisi; he heard a Voice within him that was even louder and more real than all the citizenry of the world. That is why he mortified his body when it clamored so loudly for attention that it threatened to drown out the peace of his Voice inside.

Everything then that he and the brothers had done and suffered was for union with God, who dwelt inside them. They had sacrificed everything that their love might be consummated there in that Garden of delights. And it had! The Journey had not been in vain, nor had the Dream deceived them.

Ah, my lover, my Lord, my God and my All! How terrible and dark were the alleys to You. What mazes, inside and out, have we run! But we found You, or rather, You found us. We were waiting at the door when You knocked and You entered into us and the Garden sprang to Life.

The walls of the Garden crumbled and fell, for we were no longer to be imprisoned by our false needs, our selfish walling in of things we thought were necessary to hoard and protect. Then the fragrance that burst forth from that new Garden surrounded us and drew more and more people to that Journey within, confident that they, too, would find the door where you were knocking, seeking to enter and walk with them that cool Journey through the Garden.

Brother Ass

Francis in winter, grey beggar etched into the white countryside, one with the groundhog and fox, scurrying grey objects keeping the landscape alive. Francis felt sorry for Brother Ass, his body, because it was so ill-equipped for winter. The animals of the forest all had warm insulating fur, and he had only a frayed sackcloth habit, patched inside and out.

As Francis grew older, he regretted the harsh treatment he had given Brother Ass all through his life. Before his conversion he had pampered and spoiled his body, and afterwards he had ignored and taken Brother Ass for granted. They were partners, really, and should have supported one another on the Journey. Besides, the Spirit dwelled in his body, and through his own fault, the dwelling place was shoddy. Not that the Holy Spirit minded, but Francis felt embarrassed by the poor welcome he was forced to give.

He remembered, once when he was tempted, he had rolled in a snow-covered briar patch to distract himself and to drive away the urgings of the flesh. He feared now that he had taken Brother Ass too seriously. True, he had given his body a humorous name, but he also feared it, because he knew that flesh had the power to extinguish the spirit of God. Like all fears, this one at times became more important than what was actually feared, and caution became a virtue in and for itself. That is why he now wanted to patch up his difficulties with Brother Body. Lately, "Brother Ass" had become a distasteful name. Francis preferred "Brother Body," which was more reverent and indicated the respect that his body had won in his eyes.

Furthermore, Francis no longer saw his body as something apart from him. He *was* his body; the spirit and body were one. He was one person. He was a spirit-filled man. That he had earlier seen so great a cleavage between body and spirit bothered him, and he wondered why it had taken him so long to see that even his body had been made spirit by the Incarnation of God. Jesus was God enfleshed, and all of creation was now infused with the Spirit by the touch of God's only Son.

Francis looked at his own flesh and smiled at how compatible it seemed now. How patient and long-suffering his poor body had been. With an act of the will he now made the body his. He called it by his own name, "Francis." He was one Francis, within and without. And the winter cold hurt *him*. He prayed for Lady Poverty to keep him warm.

Rain on the Mountain

There was something about the loneliness of Mount Subasio at night when the wind whipped through the trees and the only sound was the rustling of leaves that made sinister beings lurk everywhere in the darkness. He knew that Brother Leo and the other brothers were not far away in their own little caves, but the silence of the wind numbed his sense of nearness to them. How such a strong wind could be silent, he did not understand. Perhaps it blew away the other comforting sounds of birds and crickets and replaced them with a rushing, turbulent sound he didn't want to hear, and only the pleasant sounds were silent.

In the daytime he loved the sound of the wind in the trees. It was like the breath of God, moving sometimes gently, sometimes roughly, across the face of the mountain. But at night the sound changed and became a sinister, silent rustling in the darkness. And yet it was the same wind. How forceful were the dark powers of the imagination that they even changed the wind into their own grotesque phantoms.

And the night wind on the mountain reminded him of that dark side of the mind that could turn prayer into an exercise of phantom chasing. He remembered one of the brothers who, instead of entering into the cavern of peace, would linger at the entrance and let himself be frightened by the night winds of his own problems. He would become preoccupied with himself, and each little fault or failing would be magnified into huge phantoms hiding in the forest, accusing him from behind the shadows of trees.

Francis told him to think of the rain on the mountain. After the wind, came the gentle drops of rain, cleansing and purifying and drowning the dark lingering phantoms. But the young man only argued that sometimes the wind did not stop with the rain but lashed the drops of water at you and blinded you even more. Francis realized then that the young brother was still on that elementary level of prayer, still frightening himself with his self-made phantoms into the penance and prayer of fear. He lived in the night wind of the mountain because he chose to, his hidden desire unknown probably even to himself.

One day, in God's own time, he would see the folly of fleeing from phantoms in the night and in his own daybreak he would recognize his monsters as the lovely shadows of aspens and pines and their fragrance would make him smile that he ever feared them.

The Journey Afar

To be an Apostle is to be a pilgrim and stranger in this world. Of that Francis was sure. He and his brothers had been sent by Christ and by Innocent, His vicar on earth, to preach the Good News of Jesus. And it was this Journey ever onward which, over the years, had been their chief source of unity. The call of the mission to spread the Gospel was the marrow of the Lesser Brothers' vocation.

Once at a general meeting of the Brotherhood, he had been depressed and exhausted over the constant pettiness of some of the brothers about interpretations of their Rule of Life. His eyes by then were already greatly weakened and the health of Brother Body was broken. Francis would sit at the feet of Brother Elias; and when he wished to speak, he would tug at Brother Elias' habit and Elias, in his booming voice, would repeat Francis' words to the assembled brothers.

Francis lamented to the brothers that they had made no provision for new missions to foreign lands but had turned the general meeting inward onto their own squabbles over poverty and learning. Immediately 90 brothers rose, offering themselves even to the death. And Francis had hidden his face in Brother Elias' habit and wept. The Journey had once again unified and inspired the brothers! How lovely are the feet of those who spread the Good News of Jesus. And how he longed to go with these true brothers of Jesus, who had made Himself a pilgrim and stranger on this earth for love of us.

Francis fondly remembered each of these missionaries and how he had found time during the meeting to talk to each one individually and how reverently he had kissed the hands of these Apostles who might never return to Italy. For some of them the palm of martyrdom was surely waiting. "Greater love than this no one has than to lay down one's life for one's friends." He begged Jesus to accept his own suffering as a part of the martyrdom of the brothers, for the martyr's crown was part of the Dream in Francis' mind. After his conversion, he had always hoped that he could die for the Dream, that he would fall like a knight on the road, and the Journey and the Dream would merge into one.

But Lady Poverty had stripped him even of that pride, so legitimate for any lover, so glorious for the Christian, so important to the Knight-Errant of the Lord. He would be the Little Poor Man, even among the saints of God.

Eucharist

Jesus in the Sacrament dwelled in every church the brothers served, but no one would come to those churches unless the brothers there were holy. For Jesus manifests Himself in people, not in churches. *Their* faith and *their* love make the Sacrament real for those without faith. Bread and wine are transformed into Christ, and Christ eaten transforms people. And it is they, transformed, who touch others. Bread and wine remain just that to human eyes, but the people of God are somehow other than they were before the coming-in of Jesus.

Oh, the brothers! How long would they continue breathing in and breathing out the Lord? They *were* the Eucharist for those who could not fathom bread and wine as Christ. Would that every brother realized his witness to his fellows. The Eucharist meant nothing if those who ate it did not turn around and walk like children once again. The Eucharist was given for us, not we for Eucharist.

Oh, the brothers! Could they continue on the Journey nourished by their Lord alone? If they could not, then again the Eucharist would fail to be for them what Christ intended it to be. It was the Dream realized within them, it was food to make the Journey possible.

And when he thought now of the brothers, it was not just of the company of Lesser Brothers, but of all men and women of every time and place who breathed the Lord in and out as regularly as air. He thought of all who would let Christ transform them into what they needed to become in order to be happy. He found them in his own time and place, and he saw that transformation in their eyes. He saw them in the future, for the Word would always speak, and there would continue to be hearers of that Word. They would make the Eucharist convincing by the total transformation of their lives.

Of Mountain Hideaways

Mount Subasio! Always there towering above Assisi, dominating the whole of the valley below, making the hill of the Rocca Maggiore seem a mere bump on the horizon. It was to Mount Subasio and the little hermitage, actually a simple cave, that Francis had returned again and again when the Dream began to fade. The sheer physical hardship of the long hike to the top and the cold hard rocks he slept on shook him again into the Romance of the Quest, the adventure of the knight of Christ. On the plain below, even in the Church of the Portiuncula, the dullness of life set in, and there was no glory of combat, no test of battle.

Francis feared that some day the brothers would lose the Vision and would settle down into routine and boredom. They had to be continually renewed, as he was, by places like the hermitage on Mount Subasio. There at that high altitude, in those stark caves, it was possible to return to the primitive, the elemental, in nature and in oneself.

There, too, decisions were simpler. The distractions of the daily preoccupations of living with others were stripped away, and you lived alone with Jesus in the purity and rigor of the mountain. The stone Francis slept on in the hermitage seemed softer by far than the bed he had slept upon in his father's house. The hermitage was a challenge, a sacrifice, something physical to lift his spirit and make it bellow with determination to win the race that St. Paul wrote about so beautifully. Even in his weakest and most pain-filled moments at the hermitage, when Brother Body was filled with disease and infection, he could feel his spirit standing up and shouting, beating its chest and proclaiming victory of the inner man for all the world to hear.

Oh, how sweet were the ways of penance and sacrifice! They filled the heart with new strength and the spirit with a determination that transcended every bodily weakness and cowardice. From the top of Mount Subasio you shouted, "Here I am, world! God is love! God is joy! God lifts up the valley and the plain! God forgets not the meek and humble of the earth below."

And the rarer the atmosphere became, the more filled was Francis' spirit with the breath of God. Everyone, every brother for sure, should have a hermitage to run to when the heart fails, when the courage to go on flees. From the mountain top everything below was simplified and brought into perspective. Francis remembered, especially, the days of trouble in the Order, when the bad times descended upon St. Mary of the Angels as the rumors of troubles rushed down into the valley like a flash flood from the top of Mount Subasio. Then, when he had returned to the mountain retreat and looked back at St. Mary of the Angels, he couldn't even see the little church. There was only a vast plain, covered with mist, and Francis thought the mist must have come from his own brain sizzling out as it tried to come to grips with the confusion brought into the Dream by the increasing number of brothers.

Even the meeting of 1221, when over 5,000 brothers from far and wide had gathered at St. Mary of the Angels, would have been invisible from the hermitage. There one could only look up: "I have lifted my eyes to the hills." To look down was to gaze on mist and shadows and vague outlines of things that were of phantom importance. Only light and crisp air and the steep ascent and the heightened and purified senses mattered on Mount Subasio.

The hermitage was balance, was peace. He was always aware that he would have to return to the workaday world below, but it was possible to do so with joy, knowing that the mountain would not move, that the mountain would be there waiting, drawing him back. Mount Subasio was his magnetic mountain, pulling his spirit up, beckoning him to lift his eyes to the skies whenever the plain began to fix his stare in a horizontal orbit of despair.

Francis prayed, "Lord, for each of us a mountain, to rescue us from the plain!"

The Rains of Mount Subasio

On the mountain you were never surprised by rain, you expected it. Rain in huge sheets was your daily visitor in spring. Francis lived in a world of wet on the mountain, and the dampness never seemed to leave, even on days when the sky was clear and the sun shone brightly. Still, he loved this mountain, Subasio. He would crouch low in his little cave and listen to the rain through the small opening at the top. The rain kept the soul indoors and was refreshing in its heedless insistence on itself when you wanted to be outdoors walking the mountain trails. Rain taught you to wait and keep to the rhythm of nature. Rain, Francis guessed, was his best teacher in the wilderness.

But you had to live outdoors to really appreciate the rain. In a large comfortable home in Assisi you could close the shutters and forget the rain as you sat dozing near the fire. On the mountain it was different. You had to reckon with the rain, the snow, the windstorms, and the cold, damp weather. It was humbling to be so dependent on outer weather. But that is why Francis loved the mountain, he was dependent on nature and its whims and capricious demands.

The Gospel, too, came alive on the mountain, for Christ so often spoke in parables directly taken from nature. Francis heard, "The wind blows where it will," and knew that it was true. And he understood that in wind and rain a poor foundation would not stand. And yes, you go up the mountain to pray as Jesus did. And that strongest statement of all, that if you had faith the size of a mustard seed, you could move a mountain. Not even the wind and rain did that, as stubbornly as they tried.

And patience. How close to the soil, to nature, you must remain to learn that precious lesson. Whatever you wanted from nature, you had to wait for or work for. Nothing there was merely handed to you. And how good that was for you, always rushing, always insisting on your own time for doing things.

It rained so much on Mount Subasio and the weather there was so changeable and unpredictable that you were grateful for every moment of sun, however brief. And when it wasn't raining, great rolling clouds of mist moved across the mountain or settled down for hours at a time. There was nothing you could do then but sit and concentrate, sit and listen. But that concentration toughened your mind for prayer and taught it how to enter into silence and ruthlessly to shut out all the preoccupations of the day when you were living on the plain below. The soul learned, like the rain, to assert itself and insist on time for quiet and contemplation, even in the midst of activity.

You learned a lot on the mountain, provided you stayed there in every weather until the stubbornness of nature became your own and and you could be comforted by the rain's insistence on itself.

Of Armor and Mail

Francis looked back often now to the days before his conversion, and the dreams of glory still flickered in his memory. How very exciting it had been to ride into the ranks as a soldier in the Papal Army under Walter of Brienne. Francis recalled vividly the preparations for his soldiering. His dear father (when had he begun saying "dear father" again?) was determined he should be outfitted in the best armor with the sleekest horse in Umbria. And of course, his father accomplished just that.

Francis smiled now at his absolute seriousness as he stood before his parents, fully clad in hauberk and surcoat, chausses of banded mail, helm and buckler, belt and sword. He truly must have been impressive to behold, yes, and a little stiff and awkward, too. How important he felt and how silly it all seemed now. Could anyone be less free than an armored man? And yet, at the time, it was all perfectly marvelous. What pain and discomfort people endure to look important.

That moment, as he stood in front of his admiring parents, had a further significance for Francis. It was possibly the only time in his life that he pleased both his mother and his father simultaneously. He was to enter the service of Pope Innocent and therefore to his mother, he was truly a man of God. And he looked truly like Lancelot himself, so to his father, he was the most impressive soldier to ride out of Assisi in years.

The Dream at Spoleto dashed all of that. And he came home

a disappointment to his father and a worry to his mother. For he began then the shedding of armor and mail, and it literally took years to shed the last of that confining metal and emerge a free man of flesh and spirit. And ever and again the temptation returned to put on more clothes, to confine himself and constrict his spirit with material things.

Once, years later, someone gave him a lovely little basket. But when he tried to pray, he could not keep his mind on God for thinking of the delicate and beautiful basket. So Francis left his cave and went out and burned the basket. When he returned, his mind and heart soared once again to his Father in Heaven.

Some of the brothers said he should have given the basket to someone or sold it and given the money to the poor, but at that moment an immolation seemed called for, and in burning it, he had given it to God. Besides, those brothers had never worn armor, and they couldn't have known how cumbersome armor was and how useless it was to the spirit.

A Wild Canary

The free life was not, as some thought, a selfish life, for to be free was to be totally available. And in that availability and readiness to respond, Francis saw the redemptive power of freedom. Because he was unattached, he was ever open and alert to the call of the present moment. Like Jesus Himself, he had nowhere to lay his head. He had no ties, no strings attached to him to keep him from saying yes when the call came summoning him to ride out in the service of his Lord.

Francis believed that his brothers should be at the disposal of all. Anyone, no matter what color or creed or station in life, could come to the brothers as to those who care and who are free enough to give their time and their love with cheerful hearts. That kind of freedom did not come easily, for him or for his brothers. To open your arms to the whole world, you must first have withdrawn your grasping hands from the whole world. Detachment was the knightly initiation to the free life of service and love.

And being a Knight-Errant meant that you had no fixed home, no neat and ordered life. You lived instead in constant readiness to move on. That is why the Lesser Brothers couldn't put down permanent roots and claim a place as their own. That would be to dishonor their Lady Poverty, who moved about from place to place and who never stayed in one spot too long. For when she did, the honor and respect she soon received transformed her into Lady Ease or even Lady Elegance.

As he looked back now upon the years, he knew that each of the early brothers had tried to be a man for everybody, and each, in his own way, had been a faithful knight of Lady Poverty. Their very closeness to one another had helped immeasurably to keep their common Dream alive. Huddled together on the cold rock floors of Greccio or Fonte Colombo, they took encouragement from one another and Francis had seen in all the hermitages heroic examples of men who asked nothing of life except the freedom to give unselfishly and courageously to themselves. Their joy was real and untainted by sham, and in countless ways they tried to make one another happy.

Their mission was simply to be what they were and to let the light of their own peace and mutual love radiate to all who saw them. After a while the brothers didn't have to ride forth for Lady Poverty; the light of their lives shone so brightly from the mountaintops that people came to them. They came by the hundreds, trudging up the steep, rocky paths to the clear air of the brothers' lives. And Francis encouraged the brothers night and day to treat everyone who came with the kindness and love they would want shown to them when they were on the road.

Even in his own brief life, however, he had seen the luster of this part of the Dream wear off. Some of the brothers began to enjoy the Dream for themselves alone. They forgot their Lord's warning not to hide their lights beneath a bushel basket. And when they did, the light eventually suffocated and died.

One day when Francis was pondering these matters, a little wild canary perched upon the stone ledge of his hermitage window. The bird began to sing and carry on with such enthusiasm and lack of regard for Francis' presence that Francis, entirely captivated by the little bird, forgot his worries for the brotherhood. The little performer was so enchanting that Francis completely forgot himself, and the time, and the fact that some of the brothers were waiting for him on the road below.

When the delightful bird finally winged away without so much as a, "good-bye," Francis knew that he had just witnessed what the world should see and hear from a little brother. No matter who was listening, he should sing and praise his Lord with such captivating abandon that those who saw and heard him would forget themselves for one short length of a song. It was a good goal for anyone who wanted to remain little, even in his ambition to serve his Lord. And who knows? That momentary distraction, drawing people out of themselves, may be as much as any little singer can do. It was, after all, a brief glimpse of the freedom of Paradise, and it meant being as available as a bird on everybody's windowsill.

Bishop Guido of Assisi

In the time of Francis' breaking heart over the brothers' departure from the original Dream, he often thought fondly of Bishop Guido of Assisi, the great Churchman who believed the Spirit was working through Francis when everyone else was laughing. It was Bishop Guido who had settled the dispute between Francis and his father, and it was before Bishop Guido that Francis had renounced his inheritance and stripped himself, with his father and the townsfolk looking on.

The good Bishop had hidden the naked Francis in the folds of his cloak and he had felt safe and warm there as if God himself were protecting him. He remembered now the conversation he had with Bishop Guido weeks before the dramatic separation from his father. He always pictured their conversation as a playlet between a poor little fool and a wise man of God.

GIUSEPPE, THE BISHOP'S SECRETARY: The honorable Francesco Bernardone in audience with the most Reverend Guido, Bishop of Assisi.

BISHOP: Well, Francis Bernardone, I've heard a lot about you, you and your vagabond friends who disturb the peace of my sleep. What can I do for you at this early hour?

FRANCIS: Your Excellency, I'm sorry if we bother you, but we're young and happy, and there's not much else to do in Assisi but roam the streets, singing.

BISHOP: One could sleep as God intended one to do at night.

FRANCIS: Yes, your Excellency, but sleep comes slow to eager hearts.

BISHOP: Yes, yes, Francis, I am sure of that. Now what is it you want to see me about, young man?

FRANCIS: Your Excellency, it is about my father.

BISHOP: Pietro Bernardone is a model citizen and a fine Christian. Nothing is wrong, I hope?

FRANCIS: No, your Excellency, it is about what lies between my father and me.

BISHOP: And what is that, my son?

FRANCIS: A beautiful lady, your Excellency.

BISHOP: Just as I thought. No one roams the streets just because he cannot sleep. Not in Assisi, anyway. Be careful my son. A loose woman's lips drop honey, and her tongue is smoother than oil. Whatever your father objects to, I'm sure he is justly concerned. I, too, am aware of the laxity of the younger set. Where, I wonder, is this world going? But go on, Francis.

FRANCIS: But the lady I speak of, your Excellency, is not of flesh and blood.

BISHOP: Yes, I know. She is perfection; she is the morning star, her thoughts are not those of other women; she lives in the castle of your heart; she is above temptation and moves you to nothing but adoration. What else? My time is valuable.

FRANCIS: I am speaking, your Excellency, of my Lady Poverty.

BISHOP: Are you mocking me, young one?

FRANCIS: No, Your Excellency. I am in love with a beautiful ideal, the ideal of Gospel Poverty. Poverty is feminine to me, your Excellency, because of its exquisite beauty. Poverty is a beautiful queen, the woman of my dreams.

BISHOP: Come, come, Francis. I am a practical man. I am not moved by sentimental daydreaming. What is your point?

FRANCIS: I'm practical, too, your Excellency. I want to give up everything I have and follow Our Lord in perfect poverty, the poverty of Christ on the Cross.

BISHOP: Would that you loved a real flesh and blood woman, Francis. Beware, my son. Don't take so lightly the counsel of the Lord. You're a dreamer. Gospel Poverty is not a beautiful lady. It is a demanding tyrant that twists out of a soul heroic virtue and self-control. People who carouse in the streets of the city and sing of love know nothing of love. Only self-discipline brings us to the love of Christ. Our Lord never found it necessary to dream of a beautiful lady. He *lived* poverty.

FRANCIS: And I wish to live it, too, Your Excellency.

BISHOP: Wishing and doing are two different things, Francis. Besides,...besides, a person like you living the Gospel, would bring mockery to the Church. Go home and pray and do penance for your sins and stay off the streets for a while. If you can do that, then perhaps you can come and see me again. But one week of that, I'm sure, will convince you, that your lady is not really your type. Now, if you will excuse me, I have many more people to see. Good day, Francis, and give my best to your father and mother.

FRANCIS: Yes, your Excellency. Pray for me.

And every time Francis reimagined that little scene, it brought to mind a little companion piece that occurred a few weeks later between the Bishop and his father and which the Bishop related to him that day he clothed Francis in his cloak.

[Bishop's Palace. The BISHOP *and* PIETRO *are sitting at a sumptuous dinner table.]*

BISHOP: Perhaps you no longer need God, Pietro. If you get along perfectly well without him, then of course, God will leave you to your own miserable self.

PIETRO: It is not me who no longer needs God. It is God who does not need me, apparently. God acts for his own self-interest, and, as you see, I don't seem to fit into that scheme.

BISHOP: That is blasphemy, Pietro.

PIETRO: And your opinion is naturally theology? I say God doesn't care about me and you say I don't care about God. Both, it seems to me, are pronouncements of frustrated men.

BISHOP: Have some more wine. It will clear your mind.

PIETRO: So wine is the Church's new solution to problems? The town drunk Anselmo, no doubt, will be the next Pope.

BISHOP: Anselmo is a fool.

PIETRO: But he has barrels of wisdom in storage. Just tap, and presto! Liquid solutions.

BISHOP: You've grown sarcastic.

PIETRO: I want you to do something about Francis. I want you to talk to him.

BISHOP: It won't do any good.

PIETRO: What do you mean?

BISHOP: I've already talked to him.

PIETRO: When?

BISHOP: This morning, Pietro.

PIETRO: This *morning*?

BISHOP: He came to talk to me about his decision.

PIETRO: What decision?

BISHOP: He is leaving home, Pietro, to live, as best he can, the Gospel life.

PIETRO: And you approve of this romantic illusion?

BISHOP: I approve of it.

PIETRO: Well, I'll be damned. So you, too, have fallen for this foolishness.

BISHOP: I have fallen for nothing, Pietro. I am a crafty old fox, and you know it. But I am also the Bishop, and I refuse to extinguish the Spirit when I find it operating.

PIETRO: Surely you don't take this whole scheme seriously. The boy is deluding himself and you along with him. He has never settled down to anything serious in his life. This will pass just like the rest of his silly plans.

BISHOP: Then you must see that time alone will determine whether this is foolishness or is truly the work of the Spirit.

PIETRO: For those who don't *know* Francis, perhaps. For those who do, the outcome is clear. He will forget this foolishness within a year. In the meantime you, Your Excellency, will be playing the fool.

BISHOP: I choose to gamble, Pietro. But of course I am gambling from an invulnerable position. No matter what happens I will emerge as the kind father who tried to understand.

PIETRO: Guido, Francis is *my son*. He is an extension of myself, but now I don't recognize him. He is out there in space, as if he had never been a part of me.

GUIDO: It is the way of sons, Pietro.

PIETRO: But he is rejecting *me*, Guido. *That* is *not* the way of sons. I *want* him to leave, to move away from me, but I can't stand to think that he is *glad* to leave me, that he has no regrets, no feeling for me. Can you understand that?

GUIDO: I *can*, Pietro, but I don't want to. It upsets me, too, that this choice to love God has this consequence, that it places son against father, and father against son. But, of course, Christ Himself said that this division would be. God is a jealous lover, Pietro. He demands all your love, at least in the beginning. If you encourage Francis, he will eventually return your love and belong more to you than he ever did, whether or not he goes through with this plan. But if you reject what he is trying to do, he will not come back. What he needs now is for his father to believe in him.

PIETRO: I cannot believe in madness.

BISHOP: Than prepare to lose your son, Pietro.

PIETRO: If he leaves my roof to chase after mystical butterflies, I will never permit him to return, nor will I speak again with him as long as I live.

BISHOP: Those are rash words, Pietro; you will forever regret them, if you truly mean what you say.

PIETRO: It is Francis who will regret. Not me. He is my son. He must make the first move. Let him return now, and all will be forgotten. Otherwise, I am finished with him. Now if you will excuse me, I have urgent business to attend to. Good night, your Excellency, and thank you for the dinner.

BISHOP: Good night, Pietro. May God give you patience and wisdom.

PIETRO: May He give me instead my son.

And Francis always wept at his father's last words.

The Journey and the Dream

The Journey and the Dream. How they had transformed his life. How they had become entwined with every fiber of his being. He stood atop Mount Subasio and looked long and hard at the city he loved so well, at the plain below, and at the great mountains. It was as if each little plain had been gathered up and brought to a peak, offering the surrounding countryside to God. From these peaks Francis could see the bends of the road that made the Journey difficult and the heavy haze that seemed to settle in on the plain just to blur the Dream and make the mountains disappear in fog.

Standing there on Mount Subasio, the wind biting into his face and cutting through his threadbare tunic, he wondered how he had kept the Dream alive through so much pain and so much terror and difficulty and trouble. He hadn't, of course: Jesus had. Jesus! How sweet the sound of that name in his heart. Jesus ever at his side, Jesus sending the Dream, making the Journey possible. Francis knew that no one survives on the plain without affection and support. That was the whole point of just about everything he had written for his brothers. For him, Jesus Himself had been that affection and that support, always whispering into his ear, "Francis, little one, never doubt my love. I will never leave you." And how faithful Jesus had been!

In the Holy Eucharist, especially, Francis had felt this presence of his Lord. Not only was he nourished by the very body and blood of Jesus, but Jesus' presence was continued and prolonged in every church where the Sacrament was reserved on the altar. For that reason Francis had been uncompromising in his insistence that churches always be spotless. His Lord and King, his Brother and Savior dwelt there in a very special manner. A church was one of the fixed courts of the Lord, and he, as Christ's knight-errant, wandered about the countryside assuring that no unseemly dirt would ever be found in his Lord's castle. The Bread of Life had sustained him on his Journey and the presence of Jesus had kept the Dream alive. Without this faithful being-there of Jesus he could never have survived.

Jesus had not just stood atop Mount Subasio as Francis did now, watching His knight-errant from these invigorating heights. He had left the mountain and joined Francis on the plain. They were fellow travelers on that dusty road, the Lord and his faithful knight. But they never looked like royalty at all. They were actually more like two oxen pulling a cart behind them. That was the image that came to Francis whenever he heard the Gospel passage, "My yoke is sweet and my burden light." The yoke was sweet because Francis knew that the ox next to him was the Lord Himself, and the burden was light because they were pulling the Dream. He loved that image. He and Jesus, two humble oxen, and the Dream as light as gossamer floating behind them in a cart made of butterfly wings.

So many would-be knights killed the Dream by trying to pull the cart all by themselves. That made everything cockeyed and clumsy. The yoke on the other side dragged on the ground and you had to lean crazily sideways and the cart tilted on its side, soiling its wings and making the lopsided Dream look silly to everyone. Only two could pull a cart built for two, and no Dream is ever just for you alone. You pull the Dream with someone you love, for Dreams are made for lovers and the Journey keeps them alive.

A Mountain Jonquil

What of those who never made the Journey inward? Francis had seen them all his life. They were in his own boyhood home and even, he feared, among the brothers. You knew them by their insensitivity, for they were as insensitive as the outer self is, compared to the inner. And what was saddest to him was the worry and concern of those who never descended far enough into themselves to find that serene center where they would meet and listen to the other.

Because they never went deep enough, they found only *themselves* and in that meeting they began to worry about their lives, their future, what they would leave behind for others to remember. In short, they saw only their own mortality and were frightened at the brevity and seeming futility of living, then passing on, in time forgotten by everyone.

He was thinking of all these people one day as he stood atop Mount Subasio gazing upon the breathtaking panorama of Assisi and the whole valley of Spoleto below him. He looked down and saw a tiny jonquil looking up at him. And he forgot the majesty of mountains and valleys in concentrating on the delicate, trembling beauty of this single mountain flower. It stood there in the freedom of the mountain air glorifying God. Its life, so brief and vulnerable, was an act of praise as everyone's life should be. It did not worry about what it would accomplish in life or leave behind. Nor did it fear for its own brief existence. It simply was.

How much more should we human beings be witnesses to the glory of simply existing? We will live forever. Our existence alone is enough, and we are glorious apart from any work we may produce or any life we may engender. But we have to learn that liberating truth by meeting God in the soul's own core. God's love and acceptance of us makes possible our own self-love and self-acceptance.

That was the secret and the mystery of the hermitage on Mount Subasio. All was serene and peaceful on that wild and precarious mountainside because everything merely was. No tree had to justify its being there by working harder than the other trees. It simply grew with its own inner life and rhythm and lifted its branches to the sky.

This little flower at Francis' feet felt no jealousy that Francis was taller and could move about at will while it was rooted in the one spot of ground for all its life. Why then did people strive to be what they were not and count their own worth in terms of their success? Francis wished that all people were inner people so that they could look at this jonquil and see themselves.

Changes in the Order

Toward the end of his life Francis began to have great misgivings about the Order and the materialism and selfishness that he saw creeping into the brotherhood. One day he was so depressed about this state of affairs that he began to feel sorry for himself.

Always up, up, up. Never a hill down from somewhere. Francis wondered when that downhill moment would come, if ever. Christ had struggled so long and hard to be born in him and this concern over the brothers had lasted so many years that he even despaired at times of seeing the day of the Lord in his old age. That thought bothered him, too. Why did he consider himself old? Where had the joy gone that had made him young?

Francis knew, but hated to admit it, that he had succumbed to the greatest temptation of all: that of thinking that the Order was his. That he was in charge, instead of Christ. He had seen so many of his brothers grow bitter that way. And now he was in the same morass as they. He was beginning to feel possessive about his dreams again. Christ had given him everything, and now he was acting as though the Dream, the inspiration, was all his, and nobody had better dare tarnish *his* ideal, *his* original inspiration.

Francis broke out laughing at the irony of it all. That he could have come so far with Jesus and now revert to what he was when he was a cloth salesman in his father's shop. He wished Brother Leo were at his side now. Leo would tell him what a sinner he really was and how selfish this whole mess was. If only he had remembered that Jesus was almost as concerned about the brotherhood as he was! He remembered his pious words to the brothers that sadness and melancholy were the devil's work; and if any brother were dejected, he should go to Confession. What a laugh! How different things look when *you're* the one who's depressed. The whole affair was becoming so funny that he thought he'd run outdoors and do something dumb like the old sillies he used to pull to keep the brothers guessing and to distract them from taking themselves too seriously.

So Francis left the hermitage and ran down the hillside. When he reached the bottom, he picked up two sticks and began playing little violin pieces for all the chipmunks in the whole wood.

Mountain Man

It was, he supposed, that most people seemed so terribly alone. They met him with that look of having just returned from the desert somewhere and were longing to be recognized or missed by someone. Perhaps it was because he felt so close to everyone that he guessed they were waiting for him. Whatever it was, he had felt all his life a kinship with everyone and delighted in human company. Not always, of course, or he would never have lived so long in caves or returned so often to the mountains.

In the mountains everything was simpler and he confronted his own aloneness there as he thought all must do from time to time. But to wallow in a morbid concentration on himself was never his inclination, and even alone on the mountain, he thought more of Christ than of himself.

With Jesus, especially, Francis' kinship had ever been profound and constant. He would stand at the foot of Mount Subasio and wave, as if Jesus, alone in his cave at the top, were standing there at the entrance waiting for him, eager to hear where he had been and what had happened since the last time they shared the cave together. He would run to the top and leap into the cave and throw himself down on the cold stone where Jesus had lain in wait for his return. The starkness of it all, the poverty, the rugged toughness of life there at the top, thrilled him through to the marrow of his soul.

Francis knew that to some of the brothers the mountain man in him seemed fanatical and nothing more than an endurance test. He feared, too, that some of them were too frail to follow him to the mountain. They would wear themselves out trying to be like him when cold caves and rigorous penance did nothing for them but drive them inward and frighten them with their own demons that cast terrifying shadows on the damp walls. Sometimes he saw in their eyes that frightened, lonely look that said simply that they had followed him to the mountain to find what he had found but instead had found only themselves.

It was then that he felt closest to them; for that void, that emptiness, was the prelude to being filled with the Mountain Man, with Christ Himself. At that point they were finally free of Francis and ready to meet Jesus. They were then open, receptive, emptied of all illusion and pretty daydreaming. They would, if they reached that point and were strong enough to persevere, be freed of loneliness and dependence forever.

95

Of Seasons and Weather

Looking back on his life in Jesus, Francis saw that in the life of the
Spirit, as in nature itself, there was a rhythm, a plan that his Father
in Heaven had ordained. Jesus Himself spoke in little parables of
seasons and weathers, and Francis saw in his own soul that they
were true. The bright summer sun of his conversion and the heat
of the days of his first fervor melted into the mellow fruitfulness
and warmth of autumn days when he would walk the fields of
Umbria through the mulberry patches, through the harvested
wheat and corn fields and up the red and gold hillside of Mount
Subasio to his little hermitage.

Then came the long winter of the spirit when the old
temptations returned to chill his soul and the green hope of
Umbria lay buried in a blank silence of snow, and the only voices
he heard were the complaints of the brothers which sounded like
the wailing of the Israelites taunting Moses for leading them into
the wasteland. And the moan of the wind through the gnarled
olive trees threatened these symbols of peace with rumors of war
that shook the tranquility of Francis' soul.

How long the winter seemed! Even when he had grown
more mature, and he knew that this cycle would be repeated over
and over again as it was in nature, Francis always dreaded winter
because spring would seem like some phantom dream when
December gripped his soul.

But it was in winter that the passion of Jesus was most clearly
in his mind. Just as the winter winds cleared the ever-present
haze from the Umbrian valley and brought out the clear outlines
of things, so winter in his soul cleared away everything misty, and
the suffering face of Jesus shone bright and clear against the white
snow of Francis' loneliness and desolation.

He had begun to feel lonely toward the end when the Dream
was being challenged by so many of the brothers and when no
one seemed to believe that the Gospel life could in fact be lived
in its entirety. Many brothers feared that the Rule of Life of the
Lesser Brothers was too rigid, and they threatened to leave the
brotherhood. Others were wandering about the countryside
outside of obedience and some were even insulting Lady Poverty
by constructing buildings for the brothers to live in. It was when

this terrible weather was blowing through Francis' soul that the radiant spring of La Verna suddenly appeared.

The suffering face of Jesus had been deeply imprinted in his mind ever since that day in San Damiano when his Lord had spoken from the crucifix. All of his days from that time were spent in meditation on the suffering Christ and in being present to Jesus in His suffering. He wished with all his heart to stand beneath the cross of Christ, assuring Him of his love, that he would be there with Him, ever present on the hill of Calvary throughout the ages till the Risen Christ returned in all His glory and the cross would be no more!

It was with such an intention that Francis had made his final journey to the top of La Verna, that holy mountain far to the north of Assisi, La Verna, his mountain retreat. Even now in retrospect the miracle of La Verna filled his eyes with tears and his heart with affection and love for Jesus. There on that mountain, in preparation for the Feast of St. Michael the Archangel, he had asked in fear and trembling that Christ would let him experience and share some of His suffering on the cross. What followed was more than a poor sparrow should or could expect.

La Verna

He remembered that strange anticipation of his last journey up the long trail to La Verna, of his thinking of the woman with the hemorrhage in Mark's Gospel, and how she felt through her whole being her healing, as from some ecstatic touch of Jesus' hand that sent shivers up and down her body. The touch, the ecstasy of flesh on flesh, was all he could remember of that moment before he felt the stab of the wounds burning in his hands and feet and side. And after that there was about La Verna and even about the sounding of the name in his ears an almost unbearable feeling of peace, as if his whole life had begun and ended there.

La Verna was the impossible Dream and eternal Journey of every man come true. And yet it remained only as a memory, except for the wounds of Jesus in his feet and hands and side. And

they, of course, made all the difference between the poor man who walked up the mountain and the poor man who limped down.

The Devil's Dream

In those most sacred moments of meditation, wedged into one of the massive clefts of the mountain, Francis felt at the mercy of nature's wildness. Would the rocks shift some day and squash him between the granite folds of Mount La Verna? Would he slide into a crevasse, never to be found again? Or would Christ's care for him keep the mountain quiet and immobile in God's own embrace? He did not know until one summer's evening at La Verna.

He had been praying and suffering temptation all day long. At La Verna Satan seemed always at hand, ready to fill every void with his own suggestions and visions of the Dream. Sometimes it was terrible and the Dream became a nightmare. Then it would change and the Devil's Dream would look more beautiful than Christ's, and Francis could not tell the difference.

That particular evening the Devil's Dream was especially beautiful. There was about it the halo of the sun setting over La Verna itself. In the dream there were great golden fields of grain and red hillsides of poppies and the brothers were running through the fields toward a little stream. Then suddenly the whole scene froze and the brothers stood still in mid-air. They panted for the life-giving stream, but they could not move. Then Satan himself began to walk across the field with a long scythe. The brothers began to back up, but behind them was a large flaming pit of hell itself. They could move backwards but not forward.

Francis watched in horror as the Devil cut to pieces those who would not back up. Some from fear and panic backed into Hell itself. And when all were gone, Francis realized he was in the field himself, the last one facing Satan. The scythe was lifted and aimed at his face. Then Satan swung with all his might. Francis screamed; and whirling about, pressed his face and body into the stone face of La Verna, groping for something to cling to.

The sudden movement had caused him to lose his balance and he would have been dashed to bits on the rocks far below, had not Jesus saved him. The rock suddenly became soft as wax and Francis melted into it. Then there was a great calm and a warm gentle breeze. Francis lifted himself from the rock bed and saw the deep imprint of his body in the cold stone. Jesus had made a mold of La Verna from the first of his temptation and spiritual trial, and he understood that the furnace one must pass through is hot enough to melt granite and yet in Christ one survives it. And never again did he fear the wildness of nature.

A Hymn to La Verna

La Verna. Let the song of her praise sound across the mountains for all the earth to hear. For there on the cold mountain top, so far from all human busyness, Francis had ended the Journey, and the Dream became a standard emblazoned on his own flesh.

When you live with the Dream so long, how do you know that it is true? How do you know that the road you took is the right one for the Quest? La Verna. Let the mystery of what took place upon those holy slopes be proof of what the brothers so longed to know: that the Journey had in fact been worth the love it cost them.

La Verna. Let the song be sung that the Journey is an inner one, and its mountaintop is in the heart. Francis, sick and weary in his bones, climbed the staggering heights of La Verna in order to scale the sheer cliffs of his own mind and heart. From La Verna he could see the breadth of Italy, eastward to the Adriatic and westward to the Mediterranean. He could see Umbria, Tuscany, Emilia, and the Marches. Yes, and on a clear day far, far in the south Mount Subasio and Assisi came into view.

Francis saw all of this only in his heart and with the eyes of Brother Leo and Brother Masseo, for his own vision was blurred and could distinguish only the outline of what was there in front of him. But in his heart he saw much grander vistas than this peak of the Apennines opened up for the eyes of his body. He saw there that the voices and the visions were as real as the nails that pierced the flesh of Christ.

La Verna. Let every brother of the dream rest quietly in the knowledge that Jesus had set his seal of approval upon the flesh of little Brother Francis, their father and brother and standard-bearer in the Quest! Oh, my brothers, my sons. Lift up your eyes to the mountains. La Verna is in your own hearts. Climb there and let your vision be blurred to all the kingdoms of the earth. The Kingdom of Heaven, looking east and west to the sea, is within you.

La Verna is! And once that knowledge is there, you must leave La Verna, for the Journey goes on. Let the message of La Verna be that you must leave the mountaintop and shoulder your cross on the plain for the next Journey to the Summit where you will hang with Christ upon your own cross. And one day you will not descend but soar from atop your own La Verna to the sky. That day you will be with your Lord in paradise.

Of Sickness

His illnesses he always had with him. Like the air he breathed, he had inhaled sickness all his life. Before the Spirit of Jesus came to him, his illness terrified him and discouraged him to the point of deep and prolonged periods of melancholy. But once he opened himself up to the Spirit, he embraced sickness as his daily cross and he felt no discouragement, only pity for poor Brother Body, which bore so many sufferings patiently like Brother Ass, with only an occasional braying of pain.

In suffering Francis felt especially close to Jesus. Not that he wanted to punish himself or that he took delight in pain, but in illness he saw a weakness that was strength. Because he was almost always sick, he felt weak and dependent on the Spirit for everything. He could not rely on his own strength, which was ever failing; the strength of Jesus was his only pride. Poverty, too, was like sickness. It forced you to rely on your heavenly Father instead of constantly providing for yourself.

Francis tried so hard to be cheerful, especially in his sickness and pain, that he feared his brothers would believe he was free of suffering and that their own sufferings were because God did not love them as much. So he prayed always and in all places for his brothers that they, too, would experience the sweetness of a purifying illness that freed them from all the tension and anxiety that comes from too much reliance on self and not enough trust in God.

One day the pain in Francis' eyes became so great that he prayed intensely to Jesus for some small alleviation of his sufferings. And the answer he received in prayer was that he go immediately to Rieti where there lived a famous physician who could help him. So Francis and Leo and Angelo and Rufino went down to Rieti on a cold and wet day in March. The dampness pained Francis. It penetrated his threadbare tunic and shot through his fragile tender frame.

The journey to Rieti was not like the journeys of dreams, to Rome, to the Sultan, to Gubbio, to La Verna, when he sped along the dusty roads or sailed the sea in joyful anticipation. And yet this painful trip filled him with another kind of joy. This was a little journey to Calvary, because he knew what was waiting for him in Rieti. Leo had told him that the doctor would cauterize his eyes, that it would be painful but that the brothers would stay at his side no matter what.

At first, Leo's words had frightened Francis. But when he thought of Jesus on the Cross, his heart leapt for joy that he could share but this little bit of suffering with his Brother. So this trip was redeemed and transformed into joy, and the four of them, cold and weary, but strong in Jesus and in their shared concern for one another, entered Rieti as into a new Jerusalem.

Francis' Calvary came much as he had expected it would; the doctor apologetic, pained, concerned for Francis. The brothers worried, tense, fiddling with their woolen cords. When the time came for his eyes to be freed of their selfishness, as his spirit had been years before, Francis stunned the doctor and even his brothers by breaking into a prayer to the fire: "My brother fire, noble and useful among all the other creatures, treat me courteously. I loved you before and I love you now for the love of the Lord who made you. Please temper your heat, that I may be able to bear it."

The doctor, tears streaming down his cheeks, laid the iron to Francis' infected eyes and Francis felt no pain whatsoever, even though he was cauterized from the ear to the eyebrow.

The brothers, though they had promised not to, had run from the room during the actual cauterizing. They returned shamefaced because of their cowardice. And when he heard them enter, Francis began a Canticle to Brother Fire, and all the fires in Rieti sprang to life and crackled their own bright and joyful refrain.

Of Clothes

He wondered what kind of picture he made in his infirmity. How ugly he must seem to others. The scars at his eyes, his shaky appearance as he walked, his great weakness as he tried to speak at the meetings of the brotherhood using Brother Elias as his mouthpiece. People came from far and near to see him and hear him, and he knew he must disappoint them. But in that he rejoiced always, for if anyone took heart from him, it was not from himself but from the shining through of Christ, who dwelled in him.

It was at the eyes that Christ shone through. Appearances never changed the eyes. Christ's indwelling brought light to their eyes, and goodness was apparent there. Light shone even in the eyes of the blind but not in the eyes of the wicked.

He remembered some of the wealthy, fashionable people who came to his father's shop. There was one man in particular who was hard and cruel and who lived in constant debauchery and ease. He looked at you with piercing, belittling, yet tired eyes. And he would buy the finest cloth and have tailored for him the costliest of garments. Francis would see him in the evening at parties and nothing in the man would be changed. The only difference was that before, the cloth was on the shelf; now it was on the man. The cloth remained soft and beautiful, and the man remained hard and ugly.

Francis smiled when he thought of the self-importance of the man, and he mused at the man's foolishness. The beautiful clothes, the man thought, did something for him when actually wearing elegant clothes only showed off the exquisite material which otherwise would have lain unseen on a shelf somewhere.

The man was a rack for clothes that became in his own eyes more important than he was. Francis himself had been caught up in that world. He used to stay away from parties if he did not have the proper attire to set him off and make him feel more handsome than he really was.

However, once he began listening to the Voice inside him, clothes no longer mattered. They need only be simple enough not to call attention to themselves, so that the man inside could shine through at the eyes. The brothers were welcome now even in the castles of counts, and people didn't care what they looked like if only they could look into the brothers' eyes and see there a peace and love reaching out. The brothers' poor tunics and woolen cords served now merely to identify them as the little company of Lady Poverty. And Francis hoped the tunics would not, like other clothes, become more important than those who wore them.

Of the Broken Heart

As Francis grew weaker, and he knew that Brother Body was tired and ready to go home, he suffered most from his own brothers. They were like dear children to him and he saw his own waning health as the result of bearing more children than his body could take. Most of his brothers were guileless, true and faithful to Lady Poverty and the original Dream. But others, by their pride and cunning, were sowing seeds of discord. They were placing interpretations and glosses on their Rule of Life; they were learned and intelligent and had substituted human wisdom for the foolishness of Christ.

Francis had always suspected learning, not because it was bad in itself, but because it was like wealth. It made you independent and self-sufficient and it negated the power of littleness and the "weakness" of the cross. He feared learning because it was such a threat to a Lesser Brother's vocation to foolishness. It was true that some of his learned brothers, like Brother Anthony, were truly childlike and simple and totally committed to the folly of the cross; but they were the exceptions. For most, learning had become a deft tool for projecting their own ideas and their own wills onto the brotherhood.

Francis was saddened especially by those friars who disobeyed their Brother Ministers and mocked them as uninformed or stupid or whatever other names they could think up. He knew from the glorious romance of his odyssey that a pilgrim and stranger who would be free must be obedient and subservient to the will of God; and the voice of God, for a Lesser Brother, was the voice of the man who was minister and protector over the brothers.

Not that they needed guarding and protecting. That was not the point. In fact, the more inadequate the minister was, the better. Then the Ideal, the Dream, the Spirit of the Brothers could be tested over and over again. And the measure of their closeness to the original Vision was their daily relationship with the fool of Christ who was placed over them. Only the true brother could understand that. And Francis mourned daily because fewer and fewer did understand the Vision.

A few of the brothers even rejected the Vision altogether as too idealistic and as coming from a man who was overreacting to his own wealthy background. They were making the Dream something natural and totally explainable in terms of Francis' own temperament. This hurt Francis, but despite his own grief and disappointment, he knew that the Dream would live, that even if all the brothers abandoned it, the Vision would live outside the brotherhood, and Lady Poverty would continue to attract suitors for all time to come.

He wept and prayed and pleaded with Jesus that there would always be Lesser Brothers among the lovers of Lady Poverty. And one day as Francis' spirit groaned in prayer, Jesus sent another dream to complete the Vision. He saw a vast plain that was suddenly suffused with light. Christ Our Lord sat on a throne judging the world. And in the lowliest part of the plain, in a rocky corner beneath a ragged cedar tree, sat Lady Poverty and her devoted knights. And Francis' heart leapt with joy when he saw his Brothers' brown tunics there in her company. They were not in the majority, but they were there, closest to his lady. And Francis was at peace. The Vision had been secured by the dream.

A Prayer for Every Weather

On damp days when the rolling mists aggravated the wetness in the soul, the gloom of the dark and wet world reminded Francis of those days before his conversion when the outer weather controlled the inner weather of his soul. He had not really been free then because his temperature constantly fluctuated with the wind and the rain, the sunshine and the cold of his days. But once the light of Jesus had filtered into the inner cavern, he had a lamp and a fire that glowed and warmed from within no matter what the external circumstances and conditions were. The light of Christ had lit up the dark vaulted ceilings and warmed the dank air stagnating in the pent-up passages of his self, and he had exhaled the musty air with a great sigh of relief, and he had felt bright and clean and warm within.

But Francis knew that the darkness and wetness would creep back into his soul if the light of Christ were extinguished; so he strove ever to keep the light of faith burning bright within him and within the brothers. The summer before he had finished a song he now repeated over and over again and which he hoped his brothers would always sing to keep the flame alive in every weather of the soul. He intoned the prayer again now for Brother Wind to blow over the whole world:

Highest, all powerful, good Lord,
Yours is the praise, the glory and the honor,
And every blessing.
They belong to You alone,
And no man is worthy to speak Your Name.

So, praised be You, My Lord, in all Your creatures,
Especially Sir Brother Sun,
Who makes the day and enlightens us through You.
He is lovely and radiant and grand;
And he heralds You, his Most High Lord.

Praised be You, my Lord, for Sister Moon
And for the stars.
You have hung them in heaven shining and precious and fair,
And Praise to You, my Lord, in Brother Wind,

In air and cloud, calm, and every weather
That sustains your creatures.

Praised be You, my Lord, for Sister Water,
So very useful, humble, precious, and chaste.

Yes, and praise to You, my Lord, for Brother Fire.
Through him You illumine our night,
And he is handsome and merry, robust and strong.

Praised be You, my Lord, for our Sister, Mother Earth,
Who nourishes us and teaches us,
Bringing forth all kinds of fruits and colored flowers and
    herbs.

O, and praise to You, my Lord,
For those who forgive one another in Your love
And who bear sickness and trials,
Blessed are they who live on in peace,
For they will be crowned by You, Most High!

Then the Spirit of Jesus lifted Francis' heart and he added:

Praise to You, Lord, for our Sister bodily death,
From whom no living man may escape:
How dreadful for those who die in sin,
How lovely for those who are found in Your Most Holy Will,
For the second death can do them no harm.

O praise and bless my Lord,
Thank Him and serve Him
Humbly but grandly!

The very fullness of the words fanned the flame into a
blazing fire of love which Francis wanted his brothers to set upon
the lampstands of all the world, and he prayed again that his
brothers would forever be flames of love spreading the light of
Christ throughout the world until Jesus Himself came in glory to
illumine and warm all the earth.

Secrets of a Faithful Love

Walking the streets of Assisi at night. Listening to the garbled indoor sounds filtering out into the narrow streets. The padding of his own feet muffled in the hush of night. The great fortress of the Rocca Maggiore towering darkly over the city, ominous in its outlines when the sky was clear and the moon lit up the mountain. The peeling of bells from the churches. The little surprises of coming around corners and catching young lovers unaware or startling some stout matron bundling along in the dark. These were all memories of his youth when the evenings seemed to belong to him alone.

As a teenager, Francis had loved companionship and frolicking through the streets with his gang of friends, but he loved also to be alone and shuffle along the narrow alleyways with his own thoughts. Sometimes he would want to weave in and out of the maze of streets forever, touching the stone walls gently, hoping they would always be there shielding him from the future. And at other times he felt trapped like a tiny mouse who would never leave the inside circle of the city walls.

Then he would run up the hill to the Rocca Maggiore and sit in the moonlight looking out over the silent spaces of the valley of Spoleto. The stars would be there looking at him and he felt somehow comfortable and secure. Why, he never really understood. It may have been the silence or the expanse of the vast plain and the distance to the stars that opened him up and released the locked-in feeling that Assisi sometimes gave him.

He would then pray for his future to come. He didn't fear it; he welcomed it whatever it may bring. He didn't shrink from what lay ahead; he expanded his heart and begged for it to come quickly.

Francis felt one with all of nature when he could leave the city and sit on even the smallest of hills and think. And afterwards he would be ready to descend again and return to his companions.

He would be so carefree and talkative that no one ever suspected he spent so many hours alone on the crest of hills. No one but Clare di Favarone.

Years later when she was caring for him in his last illness and he lived with the nuns at San Damiano, Lady Clare told him how she used to watch him as a child. From her earliest years Francis had fascinated her. He was so loud and funny and made such a fool of himself dancing ahead of a whole band of boys singing and ogling the girls who stuck their curious heads out of the shuttered windows and made faces at the nightly rioters. But she would also see him stealing away alone, talking to himself and gesturing to the empty streets and then running at breakneck speed down some black alley only to emerge later, a small silhouette against the grey moonlit wall of the Rocca.

Francis felt comfortable somehow, despite the great pain of his fatal illness, that Lady Clare, even then, had been with him in his quiet, reflective moments. He never knew till those final days at San Damiano how much a part of his life she had been from the start. Always in the background, quietly observing, storing up everything for some future destiny they would share together. That had been her secret all those years. And in the end, only she understood how it was with him through all the seasons of his life.

Woman

She was as soft and radiant as the rays of the Umbrian sun and her liquid speech soothed his weary heart like balm. She was Clare. And she was always there just below the surface of his mind. Strangely, he had ever been reserved in her presence, and he feared, at times too distant and aloof. But she was seldom out of mind, for Clare was the purest flowing of the Dream that he had ever seen.

Her tenacity of spirit and unflagging love put the brothers to shame. She endured the cold and poverty of San Damiano in winter and she warmed all her sisters with her love. She was the Dream, the contemplative side of the Journey, and there seemed to shine from San Damiano a light that was as everlasting as the sun's. He always knew when he returned to Assisi that the power sustaining him and the brothers on the road came largely from the nuns at San Damiano.

Clare did not leave the "cave" but her spirit went out from there and made the Journey easy for countless others who'd never heard her name. She and the sisters were the hearth, the home of the brotherhood. They were the strength that kept alive the challenge of poverty.

Clare was woman. That alone gave balance to the brotherhood. For in a sense, the Journey and the Dream were masculine and feminine, and one complemented the other until there was but one. Every response to Jesus was both masculine and feminine in its perfection. So that when the brothers quarreled and made the poverty an issue of division, Francis looked to Clare to see where they had gone astray. The women at San Damiano knew the Dream with all the intuition of a woman's heart and all the patient suffering that perseveres until the end.

She was Clare. And she was there below the surface of his mind. The Dream was safe with her, no matter how the brothers' masculine impatience tried to alter it or soften it or put it to rest.

Little Lamb

Then Brother Leo, the little lamb of Jesus Christ, pure and simple, faithful to the end. Francis feared he had hurt Leo in the worst way at the end by dismissing him as his secretary and priest and his constant companion. No one knew him like Brother Leo, and ever since Francis had received the marks of Christ's Passion on La Verna, Leo had redoubled his care and attention to him. But Francis felt that Lady Poverty was frowning on this special relationship with Brother Leo and that a companion so wonderful as Leo was somehow a betrayal of the Dream.

He remembered the look on Brother Leo's face when he told him that they must separate now so that Francis could prepare for death as he had begun his new life in Christ—alone with Lady Poverty. There was complete acceptance in Leo's reply, but at the corners of his eyes Francis read the little lines of Leo's hurt, and he knew how hard a blow this must be to his faithful friend and companion. So, to soften the blow, Francis said, "Brother Leo, I saw a blind man once led by a little dog. I don't want to seem more important than he and be led by the sweetest little brother in all the world."

Then as a pledge of his love, he asked Leo to write down this blessing:

The Lord bless you and keep you.
The Lord show his face to you and have mercy on you.
The Lord turn his countenance to you and give you peace.
The Lord bless—Brother Leo—you.

And when Leo had finished writing, Francis took the parchment from him and signed it with the Old Testament symbol of the cross, the "T." He then handed the inscribed parchment to Brother Leo, saying, "Take this, little Brother Leo, and keep it till the day of your death."

And smiling, Brother Leo bent down and picked up a stone and threw it into the valley below. Francis, shaking with his illness and with the emotion of the moment, tried to bend down to find a stone on the ground, but he could not. Leo then leaned over and picked up a small smooth stone and place it in Francis' hand. And they threw the final stone together.

Of Violence

"The Kingdom of Heaven suffers violence and only the violent bear it away."

He had lived in an age of violence, an age when to die in battle was a glorious passing. In conformity with his times he, too, had twice ridden off to battle to prove himself a man. But with his conversion came the realization that war and violence mocked the Gospel of Jesus and that going to war proved nothing.

He had wanted to confront people with the peace of Jesus in a way that would be convincing. So he did it violently. He did violence to himself and he did violence to his age by turning upside down what it believed in. He wanted to be a knight. So he became a beggar and acted like a knight. He wanted honor and fame. So he put on shame and anonymity. He wanted to conquer the world. So he let Christ conquer him.

The only violence he knew was the violent, unswerving adherence to the Dream. He would let no one destroy it with sweet words or strong words, with false meekness or power of persuasion. He had set about to win over the forces of evil with the same determination that he set out to win the battle against Perugia when he was a young man. He insisted, against all opposition, that the Gospel could be lived, or at least that one man could live it if he let Jesus take over his life.

He understood from the beginning, when he began repairing the church of San Damiano, that it takes a violent will to persevere in good and that violence wreaked on others is weakness and betrays despair. The violence of the good could turn aggression into virtue. But the good were becoming weak and evil was growing as people did what was comfortable and safe to do, be it good or evil.

He wanted the brothers—all people—to insist on love with the violence of those with a purpose. The Journey was a determined advance, not a leisurely stroll through the countryside. The Kingdom of Heaven had to be taken, not expected as a gift. True, it was a gift from God, but only if you set out to win it. Your will had to be turned irrevocably toward God before He gave you freely what you came to take by storm.

He slept on cold stone in damp caves not because he loved pain but because he had set out to identify himself with Jesus and he intended to go all the way, as far and as difficult as that road might be. And now as he lay dying, he continued to rage against conformity and weakness and betrayal of ideals. He would die like Jesus and he would let no one deprive him of that purpose. He would not confuse meekness with weakness nor humility with fear. Death was the final battle, and he would win it for Jesus and with Him.

Breaking Point

Toward the end of his days he reached a new level of detachment that released him from the last refuge of his heart. When he was younger, he had asked Jesus to let him travel the length and breadth of the world bearing love in his heart for all people, lest he die of boredom in Assisi. But once his prayer was granted and the brotherhood grew, and they literally had the whole world before them, the responsibilities and difficulties of caring for the brothers made Francis wonder at times if he had overextended himself, overreached his own potential. Had he, in short, been proud and overly ambitious?

Then one day when his heart was breaking with the brothers' losing something of the original Dream, he suddenly didn't care anymore. He stopped asking himself questions, without understanding why. He now knew that questions and worry and heartbreak only proved that his own caution was preventing Christ from securing the Dream forever. He now wanted to be broken as Christ was broken on the cross. His own failure, the ultimate breaking of his spirit, his waning health: All were final pieces of the mosaic that would complete the Dream.

He realized then that his heart's last refuge had been the Dream itself and his new indifference to it gave the Dream back to Jesus and to the brothers. So he prayed that his Father would stretch him on the cross beyond the limits of his own endurance. Then his own breaking and cry of despair, "My God, why have you forsaken me?" would free him of the Dream itself and give it to the world forever. The Dream was God's and only He could secure it. Human perseverance was made perfect in love's own breaking point.

On the Road

Most of his life he had been on the road to somewhere or from somewhere, or he had watched others doing the same. The earliest image he had of his father was that of a traveler. He always seemed to be gone, away in Northern Italy, or in the Province of Southern France. His mother was the stable one, and he and his father moved toward and away from her. This traveler in him gave to his whole life a sense of movement.

From his mother he received his softness, his warmth, his music, and his poetry, for these were all of the French Provencal.

His father had met Lady Pica in the Provence on one of his many trips into France to buy tapestries and cloth. He brought her home to Assisi, where she remained all her life while Pietro continued his forays into France.

From his father Francis took his love of adventure, his stubborn adherence to his convictions, his practicality, and his journeying, restless soul. His father moved in his mind on continuous caravan routes to and from Assisi. And he continued to move there long after Francis' separation from him. He was always meeting Pietro at crossroads in his mind, and they would be reconciled at some deserted fork in the road and Pietro would say he understood what Francis had to do that day before the Bishop of Assisi.

Perhaps that was one reason Francis was so often on the road. Perhaps he secretly hoped that his imaginings would come true. And now in the confusion of his dying hours, he could not remember if the reconciliation really did take place or if that rendezvous was kept in his imagination alone. He wanted to rise from the ground of his hut at St. Mary of the Angels and take to the road again.

Or was his father dead? Yes, he had died that day in front of Bishop Guido. Or was it later? It really didn't matter now. He soon would meet his Heavenly Father face-to-face and He would tell him of Pietro.

Somehow he thought that their reconciliation was at hand, that the crossroads he had dreamed of was not of this time and place. It was somewhere else outside of time where every tear is dried and every wound is healed. Yes, he knew it. He and Pietro were about to join their hands and hearts once more. He wanted to burst into song in thanksgiving to God for this last Dream about to be fulfilled. And when he pictured God in his mind, His face was suddenly Pietro's.

A Prayer for Seekers

How starkly beautiful love is. No glamor, really, but unction and fervor of heart. Love, Francis mused, was like the rock caves on Mount Subasio, small and narrow, but strangely nonconfining. You entered the dark, cold passageway, and something opened up within you. You seemed to be hibernating in the womb of mother earth where it was warm and secure, and all you could hear was your own breathing, the bird calls and cricket wings outside, and the voice of God in your own heart.

Francis smiled as he thought of those little caves on the side of Mount Subasio. He knew, as he lay here on the plain below the mountain, that he would never again take the holy climb in his body. But when his soul took flight above the little church of St. Mary of the Angels, he hoped that he would soar once more to the top of Mount Subasio and glide through the caves, blessing them for all those future wanderers who would be wise enough to seek themselves by burrowing into the earth of Mount Subasio. He would ask Jesus to let their coming forth from that mountain be a resurrection of their minds and hearts and an ascent of spirit to heights of holy love.

Who would they be, these men and women of time to come? Little people, surely, of every age in life, seekers all of the Dream and of the Journey he himself had understood. He prayed for them and for their journey full of dreams. He lifted his mind above the earth and saw them coming to Assisi from every land and every corner of the earth. And this is what he said:

> Bless this earth, dear Lord,
> And every cave within it.
> For here will come a host
> Of lonely wanderers.
> May this blessed mountain
> Hold them tight until
> The morning of their tomorrows
> Breaks upon the crest
> Of every Mount Subasio on the earth.
> Lord Jesus, I Your little servant
> And singer of Your love,

Announce for You to all the children
Of the Dream,
"Rise up, you dreamers and troubadours
Of the endless Journey!
Your Dream begins."

He wished that Brother Leo could read his mind, so that he might copy down this prayer for all the seekers yet to come. Now it would be lost, except perhaps if someone young at heart in years to come, standing on the crest of Mount Subasio, would hear in his own heart the echoes of what Francis uttered in his soul as Sister Death approached. Francis prayed that it would happen.

The Touch

The touch of Jesus. The shudder that shoots through your body when He places His hands in yours. That touch of Christ on Mount La Verna had flamed in Francis' mind every day these two years after La Verna up to this last day of his life as a wanderer. Every other experience of his life paled before that moment on La Verna when Jesus burned His wounds into Francis' soft, sensitive skin. In that exquisite pain he felt the mystic merging of joy and suffering in one excruciating act of love.

It was a continuous act, for he bore with him daily the pain of Jesus on Calvary. It was a tangible sign of Christ's acceptance of him, a poor little man who tried. It was a seal upon the sanity and sanctity of all those cold, sleepless nights in mountain caves with a log for a pillow and a stone for a bed.

The touch of Jesus. How it burned! And how sweet the sensation of this love in its searing penetration. Francis lay upon the cold ground of his hut at St. Mary of the Angels and felt nothing but the touch of Jesus in his feet and hands and side.

He would die with the brothers witnessing the way a traveler with Jesus dies. Poor. Broken in body. Radiant in the light of the Spirit glowing from his eyes and from the marks of Jesus' touch. And the peace of his departing would seal the genuineness of their own vocations as Lesser Brothers of the Lord.

To be real at the end. In that the brothers would be sure they were also authentically on the road with Jesus. They need only persevere as Francis had and Christ Himself would touch them with his perfect Peace.

He looked around the hut and prayed for every one he saw dimly standing above him and for the Lady Clare and her sisters. The Dream was theirs, the Journey lay before them.

Sister Death

Francis was suddenly shaken from his reverie by the voices of his brothers praying over him. How long had he been lost in memory of the Dream and of the Journey? It did not matter, for Sister Death was surely at hand.

He scanned the blurred faces of the brothers, one by one, loving them with his blindness as he had with his eyes. Then, he asked Brother Elias to strip him of his habit so that he could lie totally poor on the ground. Brother Elias did as Francis had requested, but then he put another habit on Francis, saying in that authoritative voice that only Brother Elias used, "Father Francis, I am lending you this habit in Holy Obedience. You have no right of ownership of it, so I forbid you to give it away or to remove it from your body."

Francis was ecstatic. Lady Poverty had sent Brother Elias to him at the very end to deprive him of his own will once more and still to let him keep faith with his desire to die with nothing of his own on his back.

Now as he lay on the cold ground, the final joy shot through his whole body. He would die now like Jesus his brother and Lord, poor and clothed only in a borrowed habit. He was glad he couldn't rise, for he did not deserve to be lifted up in death as Jesus had been treed and flung up against the bare sky of Jerusalem. He would die flat on his back, his hands gripping the dirt floor, waiting for Jesus to come to him. Images of Elijah drifted through his mind. He saw the prophet stretched out upon the widow's son, breathing life into the boy. In Francis' mind the two figures of boy and prophet melted into one another. He hoped Jesus' coming to him would be like that. They would melt into one another, limb to limb and wound to wound, and Francis would rise completely in Jesus, flesh of His flesh, and his Journey would be ended and he would be himself. Lost in Jesus, he would still be Francis, but he would also be eternally one with his Divine Lover.

The brothers were all weeping now and praying aloud, but Francis neither saw nor heard. His blind eyes were transfixed, watching the man of the Dream approach him.

"Now, Little One, Sparrow! I am here." And the Lord bent down to Francis. But all that the brothers saw was Francis half rising and leaning forward, his eyes closed, a radiant smile on his face. He seemed to hold a precious gift in his arms. Then he eased back onto the ground and let the lightness of that gift rest upon his heart, and he died in the Lord.

Afterword

People believed in him. They wanted to believe in the Dream, and he was proof that it *was*. His name was Francis, and he lived and died quietly and peacefully in Assisi. When the light of the spirit was dying out all over the world, this man, this little man, this one man, reenkindled the flame. He was only 45 years old when he died, but he left behind a Dream to dream and a Journey to challenge everyone.

This book is my own Dream and my own Journey with Francis. My prayer is that the Dream will come clear for you, that you will be challenged, too, to set out on a Journey with Francis to that Peace and Joy that surpasses all understanding. But when you do, remember:

> Both are important,
> The Journey and Dream,
> The coming out and the entering in.

> Without the Journey
> The Dream is a futile entering into yourself

Where you ride a monotonous wheel
That spins around you alone.

With the Journey
The entering in is itself a Journey
that does not end inside you
But passes through the self and
Out the other side of you
Where you ride the wheel
You found inside.

To remain inside too long
Makes the Journey a fairytale Odyssey
And the Dream becomes illusion.
The wheel must spin on the real road
Where your Dream leads you.

To remain on the road too long
Dims the Dream Until you no longer see it
And the road replaces the Dream.

The Journey and the Dream
Are one balanced act of love
And both are realized
Outside the mind.